Weaving A Family

By Peggy Weber

Copyright © 1996

Published by Peggy Weber

All rights reserved. No part of this book may be reproduced in any form, without permission in writing from the author.

ISBN 0-9655594-0-8

For your convenience, an order form can be found at the back of this book for purchasing additional copies.

DEDICATION

To my husband, John, who guided me and encouraged me in this project.

To my children, Kerry, Matthew and Elizabeth, who inspired me to write.

To my parents, Hank and Connie Martin, who bought me my first typewriter.

FOREWORD

I must admit that I am a bit nervous about this book. I don't want anyone to think that just because I wrote a book about family that I am an expert. That is hardly the truth. My children have tantrums. I yell about messy rooms. My husband and I quarrel about things. I hate housework and my meals are far from the gourmet type. I have made mistakes as a daughter, wife and mother.

But I have picked up a few lessons along the journey. I wanted to share these ideas with others because I think they may help. I know it is nice to hear from another person -- ``Oh yeah, I have felt that way too.'' It is good to know that you are not alone in your struggle to raise a good and loving family. We must support each other, seek help from God and do our best.

TABLE OF CONTENTS

INTRODUCTION — 1

CHAPTER ONE — 5

EXPECTATIONS: HOW THE CLOTH LOOKS — 5
- REFLECTION — 14
- WEAVING LESSONS — 15

CHAPTER TWO — 17

MARRIAGE: TYING THREADS — 17
- REFLECTION — 24
- WEAVING LESSONS — 25

CHAPTER THREE — 27

COMMUNICATION: SEEING PATTERNS — 27
- REFLECTION — 36
- WEAVING LESSONS — 37

CHAPTER FOUR — 39

KEEPING PEACE: HOLDING THREADS TOGETHER — 39
- REFLECTION — 46
- WEAVING LESSONS — 47

CHAPTER FIVE — 49

ART AND MUSIC: GOLDEN THREADS — 49
- REFLECTION — 54
- WEAVING LESSONS — 55

CHAPTER SIX · 57

LESSONS FROM CHILDREN: LITTLE WEAVERS · 57
REFLECTION · 64
WEAVING LESSONS · 65

CHAPTER SEVEN · 67

MATERIALISM: SILK THREADS · 67
REFLECTION · 76
WEAVING LESSONS · 77

CHAPTER EIGHT · 79

GROWING PAINS: THE THREADS STRETCH AND TEAR · 79
REFLECTION · 90
WEAVING LESSONS · 91

CHAPTER NINE · 93

DEATH AND DEPARTURES: WHEN THREADS UNRAVEL · 93
REFLECTION · 102
WEAVING LESSONS · 103

CHAPTER TEN · 105

HAVING FAITH: THE ULTIMATE WEAVER · 105
REFLECTION · 112
WEAVING LESSONS · 113

IN CLOSING... · 115

INTRODUCTION

Creating a family—a good and loving family—is something everyone wants when they begin a new life with another person. No person begins a marriage or experiences the birth of a child with thoughts of failure. Those times are ones of optimism and hope. You think that your husband will bring you flowers each night. And you are sure your children will sleep through the night at an early age and never make messes.

The word ``family'' can conjure up such warm and good feelings for most people. It is a place where you can be yourself. It is where you can go when you need help. It is, to paraphrase Robert Frost, ``where they have to take you in.'' But home is not that way for all. For some, their growing up has been a nightmare. They have been abused or neglected. Family means nothing to them.

That is why you must try so hard at the weaving or connecting of a family. The consequences are great—so are the rewards. There is nothing better in this world than having a great family life. But, it is not easy to have a happy family. It takes work, lots of it. Mistakes are made. In a sense, creating a family is like weaving a piece of fabric. Threads split, needles and spindles are broken. Patterns emerge that you never expected to see. Creating a family is a slow, sometimes difficult process.

Yes, there are times when you look at this piece of fabric, this family, and can see beauty emerging. There is satisfaction when things turn out right. Yes, you say to yourself, it was worth reading to the children each night because now they love books. But there are other times when threads are dropped or the family fabric loses its direction. It is pulled in different ways and there doesn't seem to be enough time or thread. You find yourself in the middle of a grocery store ready to scream because there's nothing for supper, the kids are whining, your parents are sick and your job is stressful.

I don't have the perfect formula for a family. I don't know how to make everything right. But I have learned a few things along the way. The idea for this book about **Weaving a Family** comes from my own personal experiences in trying to create a happy family. My husband, John, our children and I have been working at it for more than 16 years. There are five of us—myself, John and Kerry, 14, Matthew 12, and Elizabeth 8. As we have woven our lives together we have had many beautiful times. Those moments have been as simple as eating my husband's special popcorn or as grand as a getaway vacation at a nice resort hotel. But there also have been many painful moments, ranging from a skinned knees to the death of a loved one. And there have been moments of enlightenment, when all of the laundry, dishes and diapers fall aside and we have been able to truly see what family life is all about.

This book is a collection of experiences about family. Most of them are my own. They are being told because every person needs to hear over and over again some simple, but at times elusive, thoughts on family life. We always need to be reminded about what is important in a family. And it's nice to

INTRODUCTION

know that we are not alone. It's good to see how other families have coped with problems and learned from their mistakes.

In German, the name Weber means weaver. It seems quite appropriate that our family looks at the process of creating a family with this image. It has helped me see things straight when I am confused. I realize that the fabric of our family has a long way to go. I have not sent a child off to college or become a grandparent. I haven't even dealt with driving lessons or dating. But the lessons I have learned, I believe, will still hold true in the years to come. I hope this book helps others to see patterns and helps them in the weaving of their family. It is a task that is worth the work.

CHAPTER ONE

EXPECTATIONS: HOW THE CLOTH LOOKS

Everyone begins their family life with an idea of what it should be like. For some they want it just the way their life was growing up. For others they want it to be completely different. For most, their life will be a mix of what they experienced and what their spouse experienced growing up.

Still, others get their ideas from television or advertising. They think their life should be like Beaver Cleaver's or Cosby's Huxtables. People get disappointed when their Thanksgiving dinner doesn't look like a picture out of the Norman Rockwell Museum.

Learning to accept yourself and not rely on expectations are important lessons for a harmonious family. You may want your child to be a super athlete but then he or she would rather paint a picture than throw a ball. This is a time for you to change the pattern, let go of expectations and accept that in weaving this family you must use the materials that are given. You must realize that the child needs to be accepted for who he or she is. Letting go and accepting are important for all aspects of family life.

Perhaps you always thought you would have a big, comfortable home but you can't afford it. You can either grumble about what you don't have or wake up and see what blessings you do have. It is like seeing the glass of water that is either half empty or half full. My mother used to tell me that there would always be people better off and worse off than I was. She said that the key was to be glad for what you had. If you don't adopt that attitude in your family you may be destined to consumed by the "if onlys." You'll be saying "If only I had a better job, or my husband talked more to me, or my child weren't so shy." Happiness will always be "just around the corner."

Certainly, disappointments are part of family life. Maybe you never thought you would have to work full time or maybe you expected a house filled with children. Perhaps these things never happened. But you have to make a family with what you have. You must accept the reality of your situation—whatever it may be.

I have had so many experiences where my real life did not meet my expectations. Many have been wonderful, grace-filled moments, where I have learned valuable lessons. Other times, I have been disappointed and hurt and see nothing wonderful in the lesson. Ultimately, though, I have come to accept when the pattern has been altered or changed. But these moments have come at some unusual times and places.

For instance, one moment came a few years back when we took our daughter to a "Sesame Street Live" show at our local theater. I realized that her ideal situation might not be mine. Doing the best for a child took on a whole new meaning that day.

We were celebrating Elizabeth's third birthday. She is our youngest and we wanted to do something special for her. Sometimes I felt like she was getting short-changed as she was thrown in the car to take her older brother and sister to practices, games and school events.

EXPECTATIONS: WHAT THE CLOTH SHOULD LOOK LIKE

So, we went big time and I ordered front row seats for the show entitled "Sleeping Birdie." The big night came and everyone was excited, even the older kids. "Great seats, Mom," I was told by Kerry and Matthew. Yes, there we were in the front row, ready for the show to start. Elizabeth babbled happily about how she was going to give kisses to Cookie Monster and wave to Big Bird. The lights went on, the music started and the characters came on stage. Elizabeth looked up at all eight feet of Big Bird on stage and she stiffened. Then her lower lip went out. When Big Bird came near our side of the stage her lip started to quiver. As the opening number progressed, Elizabeth turned herself around in her father's lap—where she had climbed—covered her eyes and whimpered.

John reacted quickly and moved her to the back row of the auditorium. He didn't want her to disturb the others who were enjoying the show. The older kids and I stayed in front because they were thrilled to be up close and personal with Big Bird and Friends.

I must admit I was disappointed. "I paid $12 for those seats and look where she is sitting now," I thought. I looked back and she was happy as a clam watching her favorite characters from far away. "We could have had the cheap seats," I thought again. I felt frustrated and disappointed. Here I had tried to do something wonderful for my daughter and she ended up hating the front row experience and loving the far away view.

But then I just had to laughed at myself. It was comical. And I settled back and enjoyed the show. After all, I realized, that is the way children are. You can think you are doing something wonderful for them and they end up not liking it. And they can be delighted with something you never thought about. It is like the baby at Christmas who likes the box and wrapping paper better than the presents.

I wondered how many more times in the future my children would surprise me with their choices. Would they pass on a scholarship to Harvard to join the circus? Would they quit piano and join a rock band? And would I, as a parent, have the wisdom and grace, to accept that not everyone wants to be in the front row of life and has to find the spot where they are comfortable?

When you accept people and situations and stop trying to change them you will find that relationships in a family are a lot smoother. I must confess that when my first-born, Kerry, was little I had some anxious moments. She was and still is a quiet and thoughtful child. Oh, I wouldn't change anything about her now—except maybe to get her to keep her room cleaner. But, as an insecure, first-time parent, I would watch her with other children who gave Broadway performances in front of people. These children were the type that always sang songs for company and always raised their hand at story time at the library. Kerry would sit back and take it all in. I sometimes would wonder if she should be more like those children. As time went on I began to realize that she was not shy. Actually, she is very secure and chooses what she wants to do. She is comfortable with her decisions. She will speak up when necessary and make sound decisions. I am so glad that I never pushed her into a spotlight she did not seek.

But understanding what a child or a husband or a family member wants or expects isn't always easy. Ironically, history repeated itself and I learned another lesson at a Sesame Street show. The following year, I took my niece and Elizabeth to another Big Bird extravaganza. This time I was careful to get seats that were not too close to the stage. The girls were

EXPECTATIONS: HOW THE CLOTH LOOKS

excited because their Grandma had given them some money for a treat or souvenir.

Elizabeth chose the flashlight that the kids whirl and shine during the show. I wasn't surprised at her glittery choice. My niece, Kaitlin, selected a felt picture of Cookie Monster on a stick. I was surprised and asked her several times if that was what she wanted. Yes, she said firmly.

The girls enjoyed the show and liked the part where the characters come off the stage and wave to the crowd. Sometimes the characters even hug the little ones. The girls seemed to be happy with the show but at intermission my niece got very quiet. Then she looked at me with tears in her beautiful blue eyes and said, ``Here, I don't want this.'' She then handed me her picture of Cookie Monster on a stick.

On, no, I thought. Another big event when somebody ended up crying. I asked her what was wrong and Kaitlin said, ``Cookie didn't see the sign or come and kiss me like he kissed Kerry.''

A part of me wanted to laugh out loud. Another part of me ached so much for a little girl who had come to this show with one, big expectation. It seems that my older daughter had told the little girls how Cookie Monster had kissed her the year before when she was at the show (in the front row— remember?) She said she thought it was because Cookie had seen her little, felt Cookie Monster sign which was her souvenir of the show.

I never thought anything about it, but Kaitlin hung on Kerry's every word and spent her money on a sign just in the hopes of getting a kiss. She really wanted the glittery flashlight but took the sign with the idea that her experience would be like Kerry's. Of course it wasn't, and she regretted her choice. It would be nice to report that the fuzzy, blue monster did kiss her after intermission—but he didn't. And she couldn't return her prize for the light. She was sadder and wiser that day. And I learned from that day how many problems result when people don't understand each other or hear the same things. I thought Kaitlin wanted one thing and she, quite obviously to her, wanted another. Our expectations collided and the result was tears. And my niece learned a tough lesson in life that day.

It is a lesson all of us learn whether we are 5 or 50 and whether we want kisses or something else. We envision the beauty of a baby's birth and maybe forget about the messy diapers. We envision a happy family reunion and forget about the uncle with a drinking problem. We want kisses and we get kicks. We want a daughter to look like Pollyanna and she comes home with a tattoo or an earring in her nose.

The only thing that will keep you sane or reasonably happy during those moments is to decide that nothing is ever wasted and that there is a reason for everything. If we don't believe that, then the family cloth we are weaving is just a hodgepodge of threads that will never be a unit.

When your expectations are not met, that does not mean that something bad has happened. Actually, it can be a sign that you must change what you expect. Too often, as parents or as a couple we expect the worse. ``I knew you would say that,'' a husband might say to a wife. Or ``You kids never can be quiet or get along,'' might be the words parents repeat too often to their children.

Studies have shown that when a classroom teacher thinks her students are capable and expects a lot from them then a lot is given—no matter what the ability. If we expect the best from people then usually the best things will happen. Upon

EXPECTATIONS: HOW THE CLOTH LOOKS

reflection, I realize that as a parent and a spouse, I have not been positive in my expectations and have looked at the darker side of situations or people. But then I am given a lovely surprise. I am reminded that even though I might think my family cloth is being woven one way, it really is a lovely, different design that is going in another direction.

Over a period of a few days one month, I got several reminders. The first was when we were getting ready for a swimming class and I was yelling for the kids to get ready. My oldest loves to dilly-dally and can be a dreamer. I can send her upstairs for one thing and she will come down with her nose in a book and forget why she had gone upstairs in the first place.

She was supposed to be upstairs getting her bathing suit. "Hurry up," I yelled. "Let's move it," came my second warning. "Strike three," I thought, she was going to be out of luck. I charged up the stairs and turned the knob on her door only to find that she had locked the door. "Open this door and come out now," I said with a hint of anger in my voice. She replied very sweetly, "One minute."

I stood in the hallway for about two minutes. The steam was rising and I was not happy. I envisioned her looking for her bathing suit after having stared out her window all this time or perhaps she had gotten lost in another book. I was just about to start the responsibility lecture, when she opened the door. I entered her room. To my surprise and embarrassment, I realized that she had been quietly cleaning her room. She stood there with a proud look in her eyes—like a dog who had brought her master his newspaper and slippers. I felt happy and foolish at the same time. It was a message saying—don't be so hard. Don't think the worse. Don't paint yourself or your family into corners. Don't label the children as the tough thread or the one that gets into knots.

A few days later, that idea was reinforced when Kerry came home from a church bus trip to a baseball game and saw her younger brother. Now, she and Matthew are only 17 months apart so they have squabbled often. But on this day, she came into the garage and he ran out to greet her. Shyly, he threw his arms around her and said, ``I missed you.'' Her response was a hug back and a mumbled ``Me too.''

Now it wasn't peace between Israel and Palestine, but that moment was so tender and wonderful. It was not done for my benefit because they did not know I was coming out the door. Rather, this second lesson for me was a sign that love was present between brother and sister and maybe they will spend the holidays together when they are older. It made me re-think my role as a referee and realize that love was present amid the little battles. It also made me want to emphasize their kindness to each other so they could see how good life is when they get along. But it also showed that I had to stop focusing on making them get along and just let them be. It also showed me that ``family togetherness'' is not always the ideal. Sometimes it is nice for the kids to be apart and have their own interests and time and attention. We can all enrich each other's lives that way.

The third lesson I learned during that period of time came in a very strange place. We had to attend a Mass for my mother at a local monastery for cloistered nuns. My father had arranged it for a very early hour on a freezing December day.

No one wanted to get up at 6:30 a.m. and drive 30 minutes to sit in a cold chapel and pray. We all were rather crabby and grumbled a bit when we got into the car. However, after the Mass the nuns invited us to their parlor for juice and donuts and started chatting with the children. They really were delightful women who talked about baseball with Matthew and even played with a balloon that one of the children had in their pocket and had blown up.

I never would have guessed our children would have had such a good time at a cloistered monastery. But that unusual place holds warm memories for our family. We have returned there again for Masses and visit with these women on occasion. It's not a mall or a movie. But somehow the children find it to be a place of welcome and joy.

Our trip there was, again, a reminder that life holds many surprises and that you can't just dismiss places or people. Don't think a child won't like an art museum. Or don't expect a child to be thrilled with an amusement park. They might not like the long lines or the crowds.

Making choices in life is like strawberry picking. The best berries do not jump out and say pick me. And some of the big red ones have a mushy side. Some of the best berries are hidden and you have to work to find them. But they are the sweetest.

Finding what is right for your family is work, too. You have to first decide who you are and what you can do. If you don't like to decorate cakes or sew Halloween costumes—that's okay. If your house doesn't look like something out of a beautiful homes magazine—that's okay too. What is important is to try and find a pattern for your family and pull your life together—bit by bit. It is a struggle but it holds many surprises and joy.

REFLECTION

There are days I want a "happy meal," and that doesn't mean a burger, fries and a toy! I want us to sit and dine graciously—each sharing a nice story of the day. But I know those moments are few and far between. Help me to accept the spontaneity of family life and to appreciate the beauty of each day. Help me to see that macaroni and cheese and a few smiles, can be a special time and the fabric of a good family life.

EXPECTATIONS: HOW THE CLOTH LOOKS

WEAVING LESSONS

- *Everything doesn't have to be a Kodak moment. You will get lost on your way to cut down your Christmas tree. We did. No one felt like singing ``Jingle Bells.'' Enjoy the spontaneity that family life offers.*

- *No family is perfect—even the ones who send out Christmas newsletters and cards with the picture of gorgeous children who get straight A's on their report cards.*

- *A sense of humor always helps. We took the scenic route one day and ran into a wall of fog for miles. We could have grumbled or laughed—we laughed. You should never take things too seriously.*

- *Be open to life's lessons. After something good or bad has happened, sit down and think about it. Then you can try and make the good things happen again and avoid the bad.*

- *Society gives us a lot of images of what a family should be. Don't get caught in that trap. Just love, be open and the rest should follow. Accept your family as they are.*

CHAPTER TWO

MARRIAGE: TYING THREADS

Families begin when a husband and wife make a commitment to each other. They "tie the knot" and begin the weaving process of their family.

Much has been written about marriage. But the most important thing to do when weaving a marriage and family is to keep the knot tied. That beginning step of commitment, if made in good faith, must be the foundation for everything else. In other words, the cloth has begun—there will be mistakes and rips—but don't abandon the project. Even if you have to go back to the beginning, keep at it. There is nothing more worthwhile than a long, lasting union.

Romance is wonderful. It is exciting and that first feeling of falling in love is wondrous. But there is nothing more fulfilling and sweet than a marriage that has aged like a good wine. It is worth the work and effort. It shows that a good marriage is beyond price.

Recently, my husband and I attended a wedding. He reminded me that when we were married 16 years ago the priest asked everyone to renew their wedding vows at our wedding. He squeezed my hand and we nodded to each other, at this wedding, as the couple made their promises. We renewed our vows and added another knot to our fabric and made the weaving of our family a little tighter and nicer.

Commitment is the key to any marriage. There have been days when most married couples have wanted to walk away from each other. I think that a husband and wife know each other so well that they know how to make each other the most angry. And they also know each other's vulnerable points so well that they can needle each other the best.

Also, most of us won't lose our temper at work or in social situations. Rather, we know that we can ``take it out'' at home and that we will still be loved. My husband can fall asleep in the chair and not be sociable for an evening because he knows he does not have to be ``on'' for me. He might have had to talk with 50 people at work and he had to be bright and attentive. But at home he can just surf the television channels and be quiet. And I can wear a worn flannel nightgown to bed or get lost in a book or leave the kitchen floor dirty one more day and still feel loved and at home.

This kind of relationship does not happen overnight. I know that when I was first married I tried to be the ``perfect wife.'' I had a nice breakfast waiting on the table each morning. But after our first child was born it was tough to be out of my pajamas by lunch time—never mind make breakfast.

It is at times like this that love is tested and tried. That is when you realize that eating cold cereal is fine because loving a child is more important. Oh, children are a huge adjustment in a marriage. Attention must be given to every member of the family—including the parents. However, as a marriage matures, a couple realizes that the first tooth or the first step or the first word of a child helps to make a couple more connected to each other. They share this little wonder and all the little miracles that go along with growing up.

MARRIAGE: TYING THREADS

I was at a party recently and I met a young woman who was about to celebrate her first anniversary. "I can't imagine being married as long as you," she said sweetly.

I told her that I, too, thought that one year seemed like a long time for me, too, when I was celebrating my first anniversary. I was eager to celebrate that anniversary. It was like leaving freshman year. I had passed the test.

Little did I know then that there would be so many more tests along the way. There would be disagreements about how to hang the storm windows and who ate the last of the cereal. There would be fewer candlelight dinners and more Chinese carry-outs.

However, for the most part John and I have had the same idea about where we were headed in our marriage. We both value the same things. Neither one of us care about a fancy car or a massive wardrobe. We want the same things for our children and love them dearly.

We have disagreed each winter about what degree we should put the thermostat. We definitely do not like the same things on our pizza. I am a plain cheese person, he likes everything on his pizza. I read mysteries all the time. My husband never touches fiction of any sort. But our common faith beliefs and values are what bind us.

I told someone, when I was engaged that my fiancé was fabulous. The man replied "Oh, I suppose he walks on water?" I answered smugly, "Yes, he does."

But 16 years later, even though he makes me mad enough sometimes to boil water, I still think he can walk on it. I know he slips and falls sometimes, but I think our relationship works because of my commitment to him and my basic belief that he is wonderful.

I remember when I went to visit a neighbor whose husband had died. Quietly, and with great courage, she told me how her husband had waited for her to come out of the grocery store. He didn't go in with her because it had started to rain so he pulled right up to the curb and waited nearby. He didn't want his wife to get wet.

She returned a few minutes later and thought he was dozing. But he was not asleep. He had suffered a massive coronary. She said the next few hours were a blur, but in the end he had died. They had been married 57 years.

This sad woman spoke about how she loved to read and how she would now try to fill her lonely hours with books. "But it was my husband who got the books for me through the library outreach program," she said. "Sometimes he would call me from the library to see if I had read a book," she recalled. Every word she spoke told me how much she missed her husband. And she taught me a good lesson because what she remembered about him was not some fancy gift he had given her or even what kind of car they drove. Rather, she recalled his acts of kindness and thoughtfulness.

That is what makes a marriage work. Sure you are comfortable with the other person. But you must always try to be kind and loving for love's sake.

I was in awe of how my neighbor spoke so lovingly about her husband. I left her on that winter day and went home to find my husband building a snowman in the yard with our three children. I felt like crying. That visit showed me how fragile life can be. It taught me that no matter what happens, you must always look at the value of the relationship. You have to stop and say "he's driving me crazy but what would I do without him."

So if my husband comes home late once in a while, and if his socks don't always make the hamper, I must remember all the good and kind things that he has done. I must focus on the positive aspects of our relationship and be grateful.

There is no perfect husband or wife. People argue and make mistakes and hurt each others feelings. But if the relationship is based in love and has a good foundation, a lot of the problems can be overcome. The more your life is interwoven or knotted with your spouse's, the more connected you are. The fabric of your family is tighter.

When a friend of mine got married I gave her some strange advice. I told her to ``remember the missing mitten.''

This advice relates to an incident that occurred when she and her husband were dating. She had lost a mitten at a huge state fair. It was a favorite of hers and had been a gift from Ireland. She and her future husband spent several hours retracing their steps looking for that mitten.

He didn't yell at her for losing it. He didn't say ``you should have been more careful.'' He didn't say, ``It's only a mitten.'' He knew it meant a lot to her so he helped her to look. He even went to the fair grounds lost and found department and filed a ``missing mitten'' report.

The mitten never showed up. But the memory of a husband-to-be who took the time to look for that mitten remained. It was a symbol of caring and love that she can look back to and remember. Those memories help when a couple gets upset about such things as laundry or changing diapers or mowing the lawn.

Love and marriage might go together like a horse and carriage but they are tricky relationships.

When my son was eight he was half listening to a Buddy Holly song and then asked ``Is it?'' I replied, ``Is it what?'' He gave me a ``weren't you listening look'' and said, ``Is it easy to fall in love?''

The song's title was declaring that from the stereo and so he wanted to know if it was true. I told him that it's easy to think you are in love. I told him that there are times in your life you want to be in love and it doesn't work out. And I told him that once you truly have found someone good to love it isn't even easy to stay that way. I stressed that you should never just ``settle'' for a spouse. My college professor always stressed that you should ask if the person you were going to marry was worthy of you. I remember thinking ``shouldn't I wonder if I am worthy of that person.'' He responded that the gift of oneself is the most precious thing you can give and that it should not be given away lightly or in a hurry. Always enter into a relationship with a belief in yourself and the union.

Matthew seemed satisfied with my answers. Some of them must have gone over his head. But a few days later he told me he asked me why people divorce. He wanted reassurance that his parents would stay together. But I realized the world had changed a lot since I was a child. I don't ever remember having that kind of fear when I was little. But I didn't know any kids who had divorced parents back then. My son has watched several of his classmates' parents divorce. He knows that they hurt. My son is growing up in a world of AIDS, prenuptial agreements and blended families. He, like all children, need to be reassured and taught more than ever about marriage.

I know that it is better to divorce than to stay in a violent or abusive marriage. I know, now, that many of my classmates were probably growing up in unhappy homes. And I know that

MARRIAGE: TYING THREADS

some spouses just walk out and leave the other heart-broken. Often it is a case where one wanted the marriage to work while the other wanted to grow or find themselves or be with another.

But I also know that most kids want their parents to stay together. They love them both. They don't want to be torn or feel as if they have to choose.

Even though today divorce is far more common, that doesn't mean that it isn't hard to break the knots of a marriage. No one wins when everything rips and tears. Tying the knots of marriage takes work. It is two hands working together. Sometimes things get twisted but it is definitely worth the effort to try and hold things together.

REFLECTION

There are days when my stomach is in knots about a disagreement I have had with my husband. And there are days when I am knotted up so sweetly in his arms in a hug. Somewhere in the middle is most of married life. It is a struggle that has great rewards. Help me to keep my commitment to my husband. Let me see the knots we have tied as things that hold us together—not things that restrain us—Help me to keep at it so that our marriage might be a firm and secure relationship of love.

MARRIAGE: TYING THREADS

WEAVING LESSONS

- *Nothing is ever one person's fault alone. Certainly people make mistakes but usually there are two sides to everything. Try to see the other side.*

- *Keeping a marriage in shape is like keeping a body in shape. It takes work. Exercise your marriage and have a night out at least once a month. Even if you just go to a fast food restaurant and eat a greasy burger.*

- *When you have a disagreement just take some time out for a while. Then write down your concerns and give them to the other person. This usually avoids another argument. Also, when you write things on paper you can see the problem more clearly.*

- *Don't try to change each other. Nor should you always try to ``please'' the other spouse. A marriage and a home should be a place of comfortable individual expression.*

- *You don't always have to hold hands and act mushy to show your love. I really knew my husband loved me when he got me a bed pan when I was in labor with our second child. A dozen roses is nice but being willing to clean up after a sick child is nicer.*

CHAPTER THREE

COMMUNICATION: SEEING PATTERNS

No one can weave a family well if they are working from different sets of directions or blueprints and making different patterns. A couple, from the very beginning, should try to sit down and figure out what they want out of their family life. They should share their goals and dreams.

The trouble is that so often we get caught up in the business of living that we don't have the time to talk things out. A wife might resent the fact that her husband comes home late from work. She wants him to spend more time with the family. However, he might not like working late but he sees it as necessary to support his family—which also is very important to him. Both people see their family as important but they haven't been able to convey that to each other. Good communications can help couples avoid these kinds of misunderstandings.

Also, when your are making the pattern of a family, those involved must not only talk—they must be willing to compromise. They have to talk things over and allow for a little give and take. Perhaps you want the thread to go one way and someone else wants it to go another.

I remember when we were first married my husband came home all excited about his new 100 piece socket set. He had just purchased it on sale for about $100. I looked at it and said,

"Why do you need so many of them?" I came from a home where my father had a hammer a screwdriver and a pair of pliers. I also couldn't imagine spending that much money on tools—our rent at the time was only $200 a month. To me the tool bill seemed very high. And, yes, sockets seemed silly.

John explained to me that he could use these tools to fix the car and other things and we would save on repair costs. He also reassured me that we could afford it. I remember looking at those shiny silver things and thinking we had wasted our money. However, I trusted John enough to believe that he knew what he was doing.

Since then he has purchased many more tools and the socket set turned out to be a great investment. I had to listen to him and learn about a whole new world. And he had to realize my need for financial security and my lack of understanding about his purchases. We both bent and came out the better for it. Since that time we have rarely disagreed about money. Somehow we manage to pay our bills and we discuss any big purchases.

Communication with children is always a challenge. Whether it is teaching a child his or her first words or explaining to a teenager why 2 a.m. is not a reasonable curfew, parents must work hard at making children understand what their family is all about.

It is a miracle how children learn to talk. They emerge from the womb unable to say a word and within a year they can communicate so much. I remember when Elizabeth turned three she had grown so much that she could tell us she wanted Winnie the Pooh on her cake and asked that all the ladies wear pretty dresses. "The mans can wear ties," she added.

What makes those requests so amazing is that, of course she couldn't say a word when she was born just 36 months before her big party. It's a miracle that in that short time she learned to express so much. Think back to a newborn's cries. They usually meant that he or she was wet or hungry or tired or all three. Sometimes it was just plain old fussiness. If you have ever been up at 2 a.m. with a crying baby, you realize the value of communication. You wish the little one could just say, ``I have a little gas and feel a little crabby right now.'' Instead, you jiggle and rock and walk and feed and change and hope and pray that the baby will calm down and go back to sleep.

Once a child can communicate, they can tell you why they are sad. It might be that they are tired or hungry but they will also be able to tell you that they are feeling bad because their crayon broke. Sometimes a child can't put those feelings into words. They don't know why they feel bad but they just do. It is then that we should tell our children just to say, ``I need a hug.'' That usually covers all the emotions and provides instant relief. Many times my children have come to me when they are stressed out about a test or a problem and just sat in my lap. I can't fix everything for them or take their tests, but I can tell them I love them and give them a reassuring squeeze. Communicating love to a child is like providing an oasis in the desert experiences of growing up.

Books also help children to communicate their thoughts and feelings. I remember reading a story to Elizabeth and she laughed when the woman bank president gave a reward to Treat Truck Mike. ``Ladies can't be bank presidents—only mans can do that,'' she said.

Her comment set me back a bit. I realized that she had absorbed a lot of stereotypes without even thinking about them. This book helped us to discuss that girls could be anything they wanted to be. It opened her eyes and mine to topics we probably would not have discussed.

Reading and snuggling with children also can open up the lines of communication. Last summer I read all four books by Lynn Reid Banks about the ``Indian in the Cupboard.'' We looked forward to those times of reading aloud. At age 13 and 11, Kerry and Matthew certainly could read the books on their own. But we were sharing this book together. We talked about the characters and the decisions that they had to make. We looked at life from a new way and learned a lot about different people of different eras. But we also learned something about ourselves as we asked ``What would you do if that happened to you?'' It also made us feel close and connected as we would sit together and start a new chapter.

Some of our favorite books throughout the years have been the Berenstain Bears books. They cover such topics as manners, television habits, taking a dare, being greedy, junk food, visiting the doctor and wanting to be in the ``in crowd.'' Time and again we have referred to those books as a good lesson in how things should be.

Tomie de Paola's books also have been a part of our growing up. His book about when his Nana died has helped my children when talking about the death of their grandmother. And when my mother had a stroke we read his book about a grandfather who also suffered a stroke. His Christmas tales focus on what is important about the season.

Writing notes to children or communicating in a silly way can help children and adults open up. I try and put a note in my children's lunch to wish them luck on a test or just to tell them that I love them. It only takes a few seconds but the practice is so effective. But if you really want to get your child's attention

KEEPING PEACE: HOLDING THREADS TOGETHER

then mail them a note or card. Children love getting mail. I remember how excited they were when they mailed a note to themselves in nursery school. When the mail comes they are always eager to see if they got a post card. They even like to open the junk mail. Use a letter to your child to tell them they are loved or say you are sorry. And you can do the same thing with your husband. Writing takes time and shows you care.

Children also love to have pretend conversations on toy telephones. Many times we have even used bananas as pretend phones to call each other up. It is a different level of communication and surprising things come out of those talks. You hear the children imitate the way you talk and realize that they do listen to you on the phone.

My sister-in-law said she heard her daughter say to an imaginary person "That's right—it's Weber with one B." Another time I heard my daughter telling a pretend caller that "thank you but I am not interested in your product." They hear you and reveal much when they are talking.

Communication with friends and with your inner self is also critical as you form this pattern known as family. Keeping a journal or writing a letter are great ways to keep in touch with yourself and other members of the family.

I remember when I interviewed Alan Jarvis, the brother of astronaut Gregory Jarvis who was killed when his Challenger space shuttle exploded in the 1980s. He said one thing he learned from the whole experience was that families should keep close ties and share their feelings. He sounded regretful that he hadn't kept in more close contact with his brother who was seven years older and lived thousands of miles away. From there we got talking about good intentions; how you meant to say something or do something but it was too late.

We all mean to visit someone or send them a card but forget or put it off.

I remember thinking about a college professor of mine and deciding that I wanted to let him know that 15 years after I had graduated I still thought of him and a few other teachers. These people influenced me as a person and my beliefs. I thought, perhaps, they would be lifted to know that a housewife and Mom—who spends a lot of her days reading Golden books and sorting baseball cards—still remembers with affection all that she learned.

I decided to send them each a Christmas card with a note attached. However, that August I received my alumni magazine only to read that this beloved professor had died. I felt terrible. I wished I hadn't put off my communication to him.

There is something so wonderful about letter writing. Writing takes times and thought. It makes you consider your words and really put some effort into the message. It is not so casual as a phone call and it is more lasting. There is something so special about checking the mail box and finding a letter from a friend or family member. I know that letters from home kept me going when I first went away to college. And I even found in my parents' attic the letters my father wrote to my mother when he was a soldier in World War II. They reveal so much about them and the love they shared. And now that they are gone I truly treasure those penned thoughts.

Keeping a journal also is a wonderful way of helping a family sort out their feelings and let people share their ideas—if they want to.

When Matthew was in first grade he had to make a daily journal entry. Now he didn't have to spell things correctly—

and he didn't. "Boling" was bowling and "canfar belt" could be translated into conveyor belt.

But his little book showed so much about what he was thinking and feeling. On one page he wrote, "Kippy is coming but it is raining." Then he drew a picture of two little boys looking out of a house window with big frowns as the raindrops fell.

He also wrote about how he didn't like having a substitute teacher. That was something he didn't tell me but I learned about it through the writings he shared. And he filled several pages with his excitement about going to a wrestling match with his grandfather. Another entry read: "Today I have swimming. I have two tecers (teachers) a man and a womin. I hate the womin. She pooke you with a stick." Below that entry was a picture of a frowning Matthew being poked by a teacher. Evidently the teacher used the life saving stick to prod her pupils. I did not realize that and I began to understand why he didn't want to go to class. His feelings came out on paper.

When Elizabeth was in first grade she also used a journal. I will never forget the overwhelming feeling I had when I finally got a look at her journal at a second open house that January. I had seen her earlier September entries at the first open house but I had not looked at it since. The book stayed in school. The entry that struck me was what she wrote the day after my father died in October. She drew a picture of herself with tears and wrote so simply "I am so sad." That said it all. Here she was in school grieving while other kids were jumping rope and being silly. I did not realize the extent of her sad feelings—probably because I was consumed with my own. We talked about her feelings then and agreed that we had to talk more about what was inside of us when things happened.

Communication is one of the most critical parts of weaving a family. It can make all the difference between having a frayed and tattered garment or a comforting cloak.

Talking things out is often painful and it may reveal things we'd rather leave alone. But once a family learns how to express themselves to each other it is something—like exercise—that has benefits that far outweigh the pain.

REFLECTION

Words are funny things. A parent can hardly wait to hear a child's first one. Then comes the incessant chatter of a toddler. And then there are the stony silences of adolescence. Help me to see that words can be our best friends if used properly. Most misunderstandings come when I am not clear or honest with another. Let me never use words to hurt. And help us to use words wisely. A poem, a letter, a song a picture, a hug or an understanding look—these are the keys to good communication.

WEAVING LESSONS

- *Keep a journal for yourself. It is a wonderful way to put your thoughts in order and reflect. It also will be a keepsake for the future. You think you will remember your days and feelings and thoughts. You think you'll remember the cute things your children said and did. However, memories fade with time.*

- *Always let people say what they think in the family— even if it hurts. It's okay for a child to say they don't like something or someone. It is the role of the parent to explain why people behave the way they do.*

- *Children always want to tell you things at bedtime. It is a stalling tactic. But it also is when their day winds down and thoughts come into their head. Take an extra five minutes to listen to them.*

- *Most kids when asked what they did at school will say ``nothing.'' Try to start conversations by asking everyone to share something they learned that day.*

- *Carry on an oral tradition and tell family stories. My husband has given our children a treasure with his boyhood tales of working on a farm and his growing up escapades.*

CHAPTER FOUR

KEEPING PEACE: HOLDING THREADS TOGETHER

Think about your wedding. You remember floral bouquets, cake and kisses. Think back to the birth of your child. You recall fragrant baby powder, darling outfits and tiny hands.

Now, think of the first fight in your marriage between husband and wife. Or think of the first time you really got upset with your child as he or she refused to eat those strained beets and spit them back at you.

You cannot imagine on your wedding day that there ever will be the hurling of insults or painful fights in the future. Nor can you ever imagine being angry at this little baby in your arms. But tension, conflict and anger are very much a part of family life.

As a matter of fact, you probably show your anger and true feelings more within your family than anywhere else. I often tell my son that he ``takes it out'' on me when he is upset about something. I can remember when he came home from a baseball game in tears. He had hit a home run that day. However, the last time he batted he was called out on a strike that, in his opinion, was not a strike. His team ended up losing by one run. He was devastated as only a little boy who loves baseball can be. He needed comfort and a hug but he ranted and screamed and cried.

I had to send him to his room to calm down. And then, when he had settled down we talked it out. He had not shown any of those frustrated feelings to the umpire or his teammates. Rather, he waited until he was in a safe place where he knew he could get upset and still be loved. No one would laugh at him or make fun of his feelings at home. After all, the world says that at the ripe age of 11, he should take a strikeout like a man? Right? But we said that it is okay to feel bad but that he must just learn to express himself with words rather than shouts. And, we added, that those grown men he sees throwing baseball bats when they strike out on television have not learned that lesson yet.

Changing emotions make life a bit of a roller coaster ride. Teenagers have raging hormones and tears. Babies have big burps and tears. And the rest of us have our stressful moments and tears.

I remember reading in a pamphlet about grieving that children need love when they are the most unlovable. I find that to be so true. It is when a child is having a temper tantrum that one needs to just hold that child till they calm down. That phrase about children could be re-stated that families need love when they are at their ugliest moments. It is when everyone is a mess that time must be taken for hugs and kind words or quiet.

The lessons of peace and of turning the other cheek and of seeking reconciliation are so important in a family's life. Parents must be big enough to say they are sorry when they make a mistake. And children must learn about being kind and being good to others. The minute a little one makes fun of another the parent must speak up. My son told me that some of his friends chuckled at the accent of a man working in their cafeteria. I spoke up and told him that he should never, ever

KEEPING PEACE: HOLDING THREADS TOGETHER

make fun of the way anyone speaks. And I reminded him that my grandparents from Ireland had an accent.

Having a family that is focused on peace and non-violence is not easy in a world that is filled with murder and war and foul language. A while back I interviewed Maired Corrigan Maguire, a woman who won the Nobel Prize for trying to bring peace to northern Ireland.

She spoke to me about how all people, but especially mothers, can help instill an attitude of peace into their children and the world. She still believed in peace and hope even after seeing her nieces and nephews killed by a getaway car driven by IRA terrorists. The driver of the car was shot by a British soldier and hit the children while they were playing in the neighborhood.

I try very hard as a mother to emphasize peace. I never let Matthew have a gun when he was a little boy. I told him that guns were ``yukky.'' Still, one day he was eating a peanut butter sandwich and took a bite out of one half of it. He looked at it for a minute and decided the bitten out part looked like the barrel of a gun. The uneaten part was the trigger. He then ``fwapped'' us with his homemade gun. That was his word for a shot.

A friend of my time told me she banned guns but her son kept running around the yard with sticks. She was afraid he would trip and hurt himself so she gave him colorful squirt guns and emphasized that they were toys.

I know that I played with guns when I was little and so did my husband. We did not turn out to be violent, gun-toting, outlaws. However, the world is more violent and the use of guns has risen dramatically.

This chapter is not just to put down guns. Rather it is an attempt to focus on how you can respond to pain and suffering and hurts in a family and, yes, even, evil.

I remember the time we came home from a glorious fall hay ride. Kerry was five and Matthew was four. They had picked pumpkins and eagerly rushed out of the car to put them on the porch with some other tiny ones we had purchased. These porch pumpkins were homely little things—decorated with magic markers. But when we got home we learned that our little pumpkins had been stolen. It probably had just been a little prank for some teenagers.

But, oh, how our children cried. It was ironic that this event would happen just a day after we had read a book about Halloween, jack-o-lanterns and the devil. Matthew had asked if there really was such a thing as the devil. I told him yes, except it wasn't a little guy with red horns and a tail. Rather, I said that there was evil in the world that could be called the devil.

That day they encountered evil. They experienced someone doing something mean to another person for no good reason in the world. Now it wasn't evil like the holocaust. But these kids were crushed by their stolen pumpkins. Kerry said, as she was going to bed that night, that she wished our pumpkins hadn't been stolen because she didn't like to think about bad things. ``I will try to push them out of my mind,'' she said.

Matthew, on the other hand, picked up some Lego building blocks and fashioned a weapon of sorts. ``I'll be very quiet,'' he said at bed time. ``If any bad people come to our house tonight then I'll bash them,'' he said.

One child wanted to deny and ignore evil. The other chose violence or revenge as a way of dealing with it. It was, and continues to be, my job as a parent to show that there are others way of dealing with bad things in their lives. That night we talked about why someone would do that. And we talked about how important it is to try and be good. ``When you are teenagers I hope you remember this and never even think about stealing a pumpkin,'' I said.

As they got older, we have had to address more serious matters. They want to know why a mother would drive her car into a lake with her children still in it. There was no good answer to that question other than to talk about mental illness and evil. We also have had to talk to them about such topics as abortion and capital punishment. My view is probably not popular but I don't think the state should take another person's life. I will always remember when Kerry wandered into the family room and saw John watching an old movie. It was about corruption in some Southern town and it was ending with the bad, killer sheriff getting the electric chair.

Kerry, at age 7, asked why the man was being shaved and strapped into a chair. I explained what was happening. She responded, ``That's dumb. Why kill him when he's being told that he shouldn't have killed someone else. You always say that if someone hits you it doesn't solve anything to hit them back,'' she said simply. Wow, she had summed that topic up nicely.

But I must admit that once in a while, since then, when my children have encountered a bully I have had to ask myself, again, if it is always best to turn your cheek. As difficult as it may be, I believe the answer is still yes.

Kerry, who always has shown great wisdom, re-enforced my beliefs when she was very little. She had been taking a dance class with other little ones. She was only four and just loved putting on a pink tutu to prance around.

However, one day I picked her up at dance class and she had some scratch marks on her face. When I asked what happened she was kind of vague and said she didn't know. A few weeks later she had scratches again and she and her cousin told me that those marks were made by a classmate's fingernails.

I spoke with the teacher about it and she said that the little girl in class had learned this bad habit in nursery school and was picking on the smallest girl in class. She said she would watch them more carefully. But the next week Kerry was having ice applied to her face when I picked her up. I was furious. I was so angry at that other child for hurting my Kerry. We removed Kerry from the class and she had to dance with her cousin and older children. I spoke with the scratching child's mother who was not cooperative or even apologetic but later acknowledged to the teacher that there was a problem after the little girl turned her nails on a different member of the class the next week.

I kept that feeling of anger inside of me for a long time. When I saw that little attacker on stage at the recital I did not have a rosy glow inside. But Kerry, who danced at the beginning of the show and joined us after intermission also was watching her dance. I was wondering if she would make some comment about her. She did.

She looked at me and said, ``Doesn't she do great cartwheels, Mommy? She's really good.'' There Kerry was clapping for a little girl who had scratched her face three time.

I asked Kerry how she felt about the little girl. ``Oh, I like her. She doesn't scratch me any more.'' I asked her if she had forgiven the girl—even though the little girl had never apologized. ``Yes,'' she said simply.

KEEPING PEACE: HOLDING THREADS TOGETHER

I knew who the ``big'' person was that night in the darkened auditorium. I was nursing that hurt against my child and still feeling anger toward that little one's actions. I hated the sin and I wasn't too thrilled with the sinner. But my four-year-old had truly forgiven and forgotten. She showed me what we must do to truly have peace in our relationships. We must let go of our hurts and our anger and our pain or we will never be happy.

Families must give each other new chances. They must point out wrong actions but they must let the person know they are loved.

Family meetings or late night talks are good ways to bring about peace. I always tell my children that, yes, I will be angry for a while if they do a bad thing. However, I said that I would be even more angry if they lied to me. Children need to know that telling the truth is more important than avoiding trouble. They need to know that their home is a place where trouble can happen and feelings will be hurt but that in the end love will prevail.

REFLECTION

How many times have words slipped out of my mouth to hurt someone. They do hurt—like sticks and stones. Help me to think before I speak and to try and put myself in another person's shoes. But also don't let my fear cause me to avoid problems. Making messes sometimes leads to great beauty in a family. Let the words "I am sorry" be heard often in my home. And let me try each day to give many hugs, lots of kisses and many kind words.

WEAVING LESSONS

- *Sticks and stones break bones but names will hurt too. Try to avoid name-calling. Children and adults will replay words like ``stupid'' or ``sissy'' over and over in their head.*

- *Watch your mouth. There is nothing positive about swearing or vulgarities. It should not be permitted in your home. It is just a bad habit that can get worse with time.*

- *Accept the fact that everything will not always be nice and rosy. Some people will grow apart from each other. Some people will never apologize. Let it go or it will eat away at you.*

- *Don't keep a scoreboard of hurts and helps. A lot of things in life are not fair. Accept it and you will be happier.*

- *Don't avoid difficult topics. If a child or adult has a drinking problem it is better to talk about it than to pretend it doesn't exist.*

- *Go to confession as a family if it is part of your faith life. It is a great feeling. Or seek out a counselor who can put you back on the right track.*

CHAPTER FIVE

ART AND MUSIC: GOLDEN THREADS

I am the last person in the world who should write about art. All I can draw is a bath! But weaving a family means that children should be given the opportunity to spread their wings and touch some of the more aesthetic and beautiful things in life. These are golden opportunities to show a child the beauty of the world and creation. It is a chance to have them see another side of life and maybe discover a hidden talent.

Now, I know some people suggest playing Mozart to babies while they are in the womb. I wouldn't go that far. However, all children should be exposed to the world of art, music and literature.

Does this meaning dragging a kid around to an art museum? Maybe. But more than likely it just means giving them some modeling clay or a paper and some crayons or a chance to cut some things with safety scissors and make a big, happy mess.

Or maybe it means giving them the lids of pans and some wooden spoons and bowls and making a band out of that concoction of instruments. Or it might just mean sitting oh so patiently while a child tries to tell a story to you.

No matter how it is done, the creative act usually has positive result with children. It is important, though, that this act be a child's own work. And the child should never feel as if he or she is being graded or judged on their effort.

Now my children can look back and laugh at the pictures they drew where the arms and legs come right out of the person's head. But back then I never would have laughed or even pointed out to them that their creation had no neck or body.

When a child creates something they feel so proud. I saw this firsthand when my husband got our children involved in his workshop. John loves to do woodworking and he shares his talent with the children. When the children were 5, 10 and 11, they would constantly ask their Dad ``Do we have enough time to go downstairs?''

This meant the children would have a chance to design, cut, saw, glue and hammer their own project. Certainly they had some help from their Dad, especially when it came to cutting. However, for the most part the work was their own.

Elizabeth, 5, made a little tea table for her dolls. She also took some blocks of wood and made a two-sided Pinocchio doll. The doll has a stick for a nose. On one side the nose is short and the doll has a happy face because he is telling the truth. On the other side the doll's nose is long and Pinocchio is crying because he has told a lie.

She also has made wooden blocks and drawn letters that spell out I love you. They still stand on the counter in our kitchen. And she and her Dad made a birdhouse that attracted more squirrels than birds. But it was so nice to see her smiling face as she showed off her work. And the time spent with her Dad doing something special will make for great memories when she is older.

Matthew, 10, made a wooden whale and it sits over his closet door. He also made a crucifix. To some it might seem crude but to me it was a deep expression of his faith and an attempt by him to make something from his heart for the home.

Kerry, 11, made a little chair and a puzzle. She also enjoys working with fabric paints and has made me a sweatshirt that I wear proudly. And this Christmas she has decorated a little back pack with pink roses and Elizabeth's initials. She knows that I tell her and the children that homemade gifts are always welcome and that we all treasure the effort that goes into the cards and gifts they make.

Giving the children a chance to work with their hands and minds has worked so well with our children. There are many days when I don't understand my children or their feelings. There are days when they say they are bored. There are days when I worry about them watching too much television. But on the days they have ``something to do,'' like making a popsicle stick pencil holder or painting a picture with water they are content.

Art is not just for those who are gifted with great artistic talent. Art can mean knitting or sewing or needlework. Art can be painting but it also can be working with clay or pipe cleaners. As years have gone by, I find that, I too, feel a little better when I am doing something creative.

Art can get more serious for children if the interest is there. I have offered art classes to all of my children but only the girls have been interested. All three of them have tried their hand at piano. That has been a little trickier. The joy of music can be drowned out by the nagging voice that tells them to practice. Several times they have asked to quit. One year I let them. But in the end I have asked them to at least keep trying for a while. I explain that I don't expect a concert pianist but that when they are older they should be glad that they were exposed to this. Most adults say they are glad they had the lessons. Time will tell. For now, I have stopped telling them to practice and am watching to see if they go to the piano on their own. My little one does all the time. The older ones do more than I expected. No matter what I am glad they had the chance.

Whether a child takes formal music lesson or not, they also should have a chance to sing silly songs and act out their little plays. I remember the Christmas after my mother died we all gathered at my house for Christmas day. It was the first time we had not gone to Grandma's for the big day. The children ran off after dinner and then announced that they had a show. Usually this meant singing a song. But the seven grandchildren had created a Christmas play with elves and reindeer and Mr. and Mrs. Claus. The oldest was 12 and the youngest was two. They even put baby powder in the hair of Mr. and Mrs. Claus to give that aged look. And they had gone through drawers to find costumes of sort for them to wear.

Certainly we were sad that day. However, this creative act of love took away a lot of the pain. It reminded us of how much good we had in our life. The play was comical and silly and messy. But it brought a smile to the face of all there.

The children were given permission to create and they knew no matter what they did, we would give their work praise and applause.

Families should sing together—in the car, at the table or on a hike. Scrap materials should be recycled so that art projects abound. All the work should be proudly displayed for a while, anyway. Few children will grow up to be great artists or composers. But all who are exposed to the arts and are comfortable with that world will be better because of those experiences.

REFLECTION

When the playdough has dried up into little bits in the carpet and the crayons have marked the table, let me take a deep breath and rejoice. Let me praise the 64 colors and all that they can do. Let me be glad to hear the alphabet sung over and over and over again. Let me hang those scraps of paper with more glue than paper on my wall proudly. Let me see the beauty of this kind of art. Give me patience to listen to some off notes on a trumpet. Let me be enthusiastic as they put on a play that could use a little more rehearsing. These golden threads in a family are what make it sparkle. Let them shine!

WEAVING LESSONS

- *Never think that the arts are for the rich or the highly educated. Music, literature and art can touch everyone and come from everyone.*

- *Take advantage of opportunities for cultural enrichment. Go to story hours at libraries, bookstores and malls. Most of them are free.*

- *Instead of buying one more toy at Christmas—take your children to a play or musical. Or see if your school can bring in some form of enriching entertainment.*

- *Let your child try a dance or music or art class. Craft stores offer inexpensive workshops. If formal instruction is not for your child, then let them dance to their own music and have fun.*

- *Always have paper and glue and crayons around. You never know what a child will make.*

- *Sit and listen to some instrumental music with a child and ask them what they hear or think or feel. Do not correct them. What they hear is what they hear.*

- *Wear your necklace made from macaroni noodles with pride. Display their ceramic statues with gold glitter paint in a special spot. Acknowledge their effort.*

CHAPTER SIX

LESSONS FROM CHILDREN: LITTLE WEAVERS

Mom and Dad do not always know best. This does not mean that we are the foolish people you see on television. We do not have to live in a family with smart aleck kids who throw one-liners at their silly parents.

But parents must be open to the ways the mind of a child works. They must listen to them in their quiet moments and realize that parents are the primary but not the only teachers in the world.

My children have taught me so many things along the way. I will always remember one rainy day when Kerry, our oldest, was just a toddler. It was raining and her baby brother was napping. I had hoped to go out with them for a walk or at least get a little exercise. I was not feeling cheerful, nor was I thrilled with the rain.

Kerry walked into the kitchen and looked out the window. ``Look,'' she said, with excitement in her voice. ``Look at how the raindrops run down the window.'' We sat there and watched the drops trickle down the pane. It was a lovely sight to behold. We then talked about rain and how important it was. And then we said we were glad that we were sheltered from it. We headed to the couch to snuggle and read. But I learned much from that baby. She had reminded me how

WEAVING A FAMILY

important it is to enjoy simple things and see beauty in the world around me.

She made me sit up an take notice of a the rain drops. They were not things to be minded. Rather they were lovely droplets that made funny noises and had shiny, strange shapes. They also made big puddles and sometimes they even made a rainbow. Children can take ordinary things and get so excited about them.

When it begins to snow we think about driving in bad weather and the kids try to catch snowflakes on their tongues. We see a pile of sand, they see the start of a castle. We see a schedule, they see endless days. We worry about a clean house and they want you to just stop and listen to them.

Recently, we were waiting at an airport for my husband. He was returning from a business trip. Most people had bored, tired looks on their faces. They seemed weary of the beehive activity at the airport. But several small children relished being there—including my own. They watched the luggage handlers and the grounds crew with rapt attention. They all cheered when the flight landed and everyone could hear the kids talking about their daddy's plane arriving. The atmosphere got a little different in the airport at that time. The children had begun to transform it into a place of wonder and love instead of a giant waiting room. Their openness and enthusiasm made the difference.

There are so many times when my children have opened my eyes to the world around me and made a difference. They have made me stop and look at the shapes of clouds. They have invited me to feel the crunchy leaves under my feet in fall. And they have re-acquainted me with the fun of catching snowflakes on my tongue. They even called me outside one

LESSONS FROM CHILDREN: LITTLE WEAVERS

day when I was mopping the kitchen floor to see a rainbow. I am glad I went.

I also remember the day Elizabeth came home from a train show with her Dad. She had seen many model trains and was describing them. Then we transformed the sofa into a train and took a ride. We didn't go very far but I shared in her imagination and felt a little closer to her that day. Sure we made the room a bit sloppy. Yes, there were a million "practical" things I should have been doing. But it was a great ride.

Children don't just teach people about the good things in life. They also have the honesty to bring up uncomfortable topics. I remember when Matthew and I were driving to a soccer game. He had just turned eight and he was kind of quiet in the car. I mentioned to him how much I loved the fall and the beautiful colors on the trees. He looked at me and with a serious voice and asked, "Do you think the leaves mind falling each year?"

Wow, usually he just wants to know what is for supper. But today our quiet ride gave him the chance to think and talk. I told him I didn't know if the leaves minded coming down every fall. "But they certainly go out with a burst of glory," I added. Of course, I had muddied the waters. He then wanted to know what "a burst of glory" was. So I told him that the leaves had to die each year but that they gave the world a beautiful gift as they fell. They just don't just wimp down from the tree but they give a gift to the world as they go. "They shout to the world who they are," I said. "It's like the leaves have had a reason or purpose for living," I added.

"Yeah, and even when they fall and they're on the ground a kid could use them as an art project," he said. "Or you could run through them or jump in them," he said.

``Anyway, those leaves had a whole year to live on that tree and they must know what happens,'' he said.

I had visions of all of these leaves whispering to each other on the branches about what was ahead for them. Once again my son had made me take a look at the world through his eyes. He helped me to re-affirm my belief that life has meaning and purpose and even the falling leaves have their role. But that conversation also showed me to never underestimate children. They might be young and they might not know their multiplication tables, but they think deep thoughts and say things that reveal truths about life and death.

Sometimes they will say something like, ``I don't think that person likes me.'' I want to hug them and assure them they are mistaken. But sometimes I have to say, ``why do you feel that way?'' It might be a misunderstanding that can be corrected. But once in a while the child is right on the money and we have to talk about how everyone is not going to like or appreciate everyone else.

Children also are a reminder that life is precious. Can you remember the first poem your child ever wrote? It was probably a simple little rhyme. Elizabeth wrote ``I'm sailing on the sea, so grateful for me.'' I will never forget it because it seemed like just a short time before that she was saying ba ba ba and da da da.

They freeze time for you and make you focus on today. Few children worry about the future. And they usually just look to the past for pleasure—not remorse. Their enthusiasm for life shouts to the world that today, and life itself, are to be appreciated.

Elizabeth also has reminded me of a valuable lesson in life when she was being quite annoying. Oh she could drive me crazy when she was being so fussy about how her socks fit—she didn't want any ``bubbles'' in her toes when she was little. And she still has a hard time making up her mind and frets over whether she should wear a purple or green shirt. But on this day she was annoying me because she just wouldn't be quiet. I was trying to work on the computer and needed the time to think. I believe in giving children attention but they also have to learn that they are not the center of the universe. So I told this curly-haired, four-year-old to be still. Then I gave her a snack.

She then took a bite from the cookie and said, ``What do you think this cookie looks like now?'' I answered, ``Maybe the moon.'' ``Maybe,'' she said. ``Or maybe it looks like a tear. Wouldn't that be funny to have a tear coming from your eye that was really a cookie,'' she said. She then rattled on about ``I know why they call it upstairs—because they have stairs you go up to get there.'' She continued with other silly observations. Was she ever a chatterbox that day.

So, I tried to keep her quiet with some paper and crayons. No luck. ``Do think these look like hands? What color should I make these hands?'' she asked as she drew some sort of person. I told her yellow. ``Well who has hands that color? Maybe Big Bird that's who. No, that's silly he has feathers and wings not hands. Oh well, what color do you get when you color over the yellow with the blue? Green. Right? Now who has green hands?'' she asked.

And so her chatter continued. I realized that she was probably talking so much because I wasn't giving her much attention. And I was so distracted because I had work to do and on that very day my mother had a major stroke that left her practically speechless. I was so absorbed in that loss that I wasn't really focusing on my little girl. And then all of it hit me in a very painful but ironic way. The very thing my mother had lost—the gift of speech—was what Elizabeth was enjoying like crazy. I realized that I should cherish her talking and thank God she is not autistic. Certainly, she has learned that there is a time for silence in one's life, like at church and school. But she also should not be afraid to express herself. I learned that day that the talk of a loved can be music to one's ears. Her talking took on a whole new meaning and made me see how important it is when we do talk to each other. And that day I ached at the same time to hear my mother's voice again. (Sadly, she learned to say just a few words but she never recovered fully and died six weeks later.)

Yes, children can open our eyes and hearts to so many things. Just try sharing five cookies with three children. Now there is a lesson in fairness. Kids will show you what is right so often. They won't let you get away with little white lies to telephone solicitors. ``Why did you say you couldn't talk right now? You're not very busy,'' they ask.

And no matter how much I think I know my children they come out with something that keeps me on my toes. When Kerry was eight she asked, ``Mom, how come all the ladies on game show who turn letters and show prizes have blonde hair?'' This was a thoughtful question from a little girl with beautiful dark hair.

A few days later Matthew noted that ``only cool guys wore pierced earrings.'' Somehow, through television or magazines my children had absorbed an image that was being portrayed in the world. Glamorous women are blonde. Tough, cool guys have an earring. They can recite the jingle for McDonald's and know what shoe is supposedly the best to wear for basketball.

Their comments have showed me that they are being bombarded with so many subtle messages about life and the

LESSONS FROM CHILDREN: LITTLE WEAVERS

world they are in. It is the role of a parent to draw out their thoughts, learn from most of them and help them with their questions and misconceptions. I still remember when Kerry asked me if a black person could marry a white person. I couldn't believe her question but she just hadn't seen too many inter-racial relationships by age 6. And Matthew wanted to know when he was seven why so many minorities were in a prison yard we passed by in a neighboring state. His question led to a big discussion about poverty and drugs and prejudice. Oh, how they make us think and learn each day.

Children need to know that you are open to their questions. And children need to know that you respect their thoughts. I try and tell my three children how grateful I am when they have reminded me of a good lesson in life. And I try to help them sort out their mini-lessons as they face each new day.

REFLECTION

The classroom of life has many lessons and teachers. Let me never forget how much I can learn from my little ones. Help me not to rush them when they are trying to tie a shoe. And help me to listen to them when they ask for a day to do nothing. Let me see the world through their eyes and remember the joy and pain of growing up. And let me thank them when they once again open my eyes to the world I call home.

WEAVING LESSONS

- *Just because you are the Mommy or Daddy does not mean you have to have all of the answers. It's okay to say you'll look something up. It's even better to thank a child because they taught you something.*

- *You do have the time to do what matters. The kitchen floor will be dirty again but your child might not want always want to tell you about his day at school.*

- *Little ones speak the truth so listen—even if they tell you the back of your thighs remind them of Jell-O. And listen carefully if they tell you they don't like a certain person. There might be a very good reason. Pay attention.*

- *Get down on the floor and see the world from where your child sits. Imagine how they see and hear things.*

- *Play in a child-parent soccer game and realize how hard it is to kick the ball and run. You won't be yelling from the sidelines at the next game. I tried playing the piano one day and realized just how difficult it is!*

CHAPTER SEVEN

MATERIALISM: SILK THREADS

The scene in the store was awful. The mother was holding some pants up for her son. The boy, who looked to be about 10 or 11, said he didn't want them. ``Why can't you buy me these?'' he said pointing to another rack. The mother quietly said that they were too expensive. ``Why are you so cheap?'' he responded in a loud voice that was guaranteed to embarrass his mother. ``All my friends have these pants,'' he added.

We witnessed that scene just this summer when we were doing our back-to-school shopping. I ached for the mother in the store. And I wondered if the boy thought he could intimidate her into buying something by being so loud and obnoxious. My son, Matthew, who was about the same age as the boy, looked a the youngster in disbelief. He has had his moments but so far he has not bought into the notion of having to have the right clothes. I suppose the fact that he wears uniforms to school does help.

Still, I know that I will encounter his or my daughters' feelings on ``the right clothes'' or the right car or shoes or place someday. It is something that many families will encounter as they weave their family. Each time the parents and children must decide when enough is enough and what is important in terms of material things. The silk threads will have to be woven carefully into a family's life.

One of the big times a family encounters materialism is at Christmas. A lot of people think that more is better. Parents also don't want their kids to be disappointed on Christmas morning so they run from store to mall to shop to make Christmas perfect for their children.

I remember when Kerry was little and the Cabbage Patch craze was on. Adults were literally shoving each other to the ground to get these dolls. Sure they were cute, but people were lining up outside of stores for hours to purchase one of them and even getting angry or violent. I don't think anyone meant any harm during this craze. But it would have been nice if a person could have stepped outside of this situation and asked if this is what Christmas is all about. Am I celebrating the season while throwing elbows in the toy aisle? And do you think that a child's Christmas would have been ruined if they didn't get one of those dolls? The day would still be merry if the parents explained that not everyone could get one. And if the emphasis on Christmas is taken away from ``what I want,'' then things are a lot easier.

I hear parents saying in October that their children have already started their lists. Some say their kids are high tech and write it upon the computer. Others circle items in catalogues or advertisements. Sure it is fun to anticipate. But it also is a bit much to think about things like that so early. And as most parents know, the child will change his or her mind on the day before Christmas and figure that Santa can get this new present easily. It's okay to ask what a child wants for Christmas. But the child must realize that it is only a suggested list and that they will not receive every item.

Children need to know from the earliest point in life that they cannot have everything they want. They need to hear ``No, dear, we can't afford it.'' Or they need to hear ``No, dear, you don't need that." Children and adults need to have limits on their appetite for things. It is not always easy. All of us like the thrill of getting something new. But we must not let this rule our lives. An old car, a smaller house, a comfortable pair of shoes—these are not bad things. It is only advertisers that want us to think that way.

Still, giving up things is hard. And donating to charity must be a habit that is learned. When Kerry and Matthew were 6 and 7, I asked them to sort through their toys and pick out some things for "poor children." We do it each season with their clothes and I wanted them to try and start doing it each year with their toys. That year I asked them to really look into their hearts and see if there was something really nice they could give away—not some old or broken toy. We went through their toy box and found several items but then I sent them to their rooms. I asked them to find something there—like a nice stuffed animal.

I thought this would be a good lesson in charity. On this day, though, the kids were having troubles. Matthew, who often would give money to people just because he thinks they are nice, returned from his room with a toy that came from a fast food meal. Kerry came downstairs a few minutes later looking sheepish and said there was 'nothin" in her room she could give away.

I looked at them with a bit of disappointment. I told them how blessed they were and asked them to think about how much they had. Then I told them of a friend of mine who had visited Central America. While there a little boy had asked her for the postage stamp off of her letter. The stamp had a picture of an airplane on it and the boy wanted to use the airplane stamp as a toy to fly.

WEAVING A FAMILY

``All that little boy had for a toy was a stamp. He had fun with it—but imagine how much more you have,'' I said. Now, I know some people don't like to use guilt as a motivation. However, I think it can be effective. And I think that if most of us did think about how much we had then we would see the world differently.

Matthew returned with a few toys but Kerry said that every time she looked at her stuffed animals or keepsakes she thought of the people who gave them to her or where she got them and she couldn't part with them. That was a good lesson for me. I realized that this did not mean she was selfish. Rather, it showed that she appreciated what she had. It showed me that owning or having things is not bad in itself. Actually, it is your attitude about things that matters. Do you judge someone to be a better person because they drive a fancy car? Do designer clothes mean the person is nicer? Does money make for happiness?

Every day, for families, it is a challenge to deal with money and material issues. Maybe your child wants to take up skiing but you realize it is an expensive sport. Maybe you wonder if you should work two jobs. Does the extra income help when you are spending time away from your family. And what do families do about holidays, birthdays and other times when material things are bought?

First, you should establish that there is nothing wrong with nice things or gifts. Everyone has something special they collect or like. I happen to love Waterford crystal and was lucky enough to get some pieces for our wedding. Could I live without it? Yes. Do I feel guilty because I have it? No.

However, the crystal is not the focus of my life. It is not who I am. The important thing is to be comfortable with who you are and not be influenced by advertisers and society. Driving a

MATERIALISM: SILK THREADS

sports car will not change me—other than the fact that I could squeeze into a few more parking places. Wearing $100 sneakers does not necessarily make a child play basketball better.

Look at yourself and your family's life and decide what you are about and in what you want to invest your resources. I remember one night when I sat downstairs in our kitchen and had a rare quiet moment. I had just packed lunches and was making myself a cup of tea. I looked around my room and chuckled. Yes, the kitchen was lovely because my husband had installed new cabinets and a countertop. But my kitchen did not look like something out of a home magazine.

On my refrigerator was a school lunch menu, art projects, magnetic alphabet letters, a party invitation, a newspaper article, school forms and notes from the children. The shiny new countertop held two lunch boxes, water bottles from soccer, a pencil with a hairy creature as its eraser, a soggy candy apple, some soup labels for a school collection, a Halloween bag, some cookies and my tea mug.

Now, I know these items have never been featured in a model kitchen in House Beautiful. But as I sat in my homey kitchen I just smiled and enjoyed this clutter. I know that the next day the lunch boxes will be gone and the water bottles will be put away. I also knew that something else will creep in to take their place. This kitchen is who we are and where we are in life. It is a reflection of us and I could not pretend otherwise.

It is important to let your children know that they must be comfortable with who they are and not let things or clothes define them. Once, Matthew went to visit a little boy's house in first grade. The boy was an only child and had a VCR, video game and television in his room. Matthew was in awe of the electronic paradise. I told him that it was nice that the little boy had those things but that he didn't need them and he wouldn't get them even if we could afford them. This was a subtle but important message to him about what we thought we should put our money and energies into.

Money can be a funny thing with kids. Some are savers while others let those coins burn a hole in their pockets. Some think money is powerful and important while others couldn't care less. Matthew has always liked the jingle of coins and the feel of bills. He saves and sees money as something useful. He likes to drop some of his own money into the collection at church. But one day, when he was five he tried to ``buy off'' his father by offering him some pennies if his Dad would let him watch a video.

We tried to explain to him that you can't buy everything you want with money. He looked at us in a surprised way. Then he and his six-year-old sister asked ``What can't money buy?'' We told them that money could not buy good health or love or self-esteem. They seemed to understand a little but I saw that they still perceived money to be something powerful and wonderful.

Since that time they have done yard work and become baby sitters so they know more about money. And in a beautiful but sad way they have come to learn what I was trying to tell them back then. They saw it as they watched one of their beloved grandfathers die from cancer. My Dad, who never cared about his wardrobe or car, faced his death with dignity and grace.

I said to the kids, ``What would a million dollars in the bank do for Grandpa right now? What good would a shiny car in the driveway be? What if he had fancy suits in his closet or a huge house? Would it matter?'' They could easily say that none of it mattered. It was obvious that what mattered the most to my father as he was dying was his faith and his family. Those are

MATERIALISM: SILK THREADS

two things that come without a price tag. He was able to be brave and peaceful about his death because he was surrounded by people and a God who loved him.

Still each day is a struggle with the material world. There was the day Kerry wanted a toy smooshie and she spent all of her allowance for the $5 toy that was exciting the first day and lay on the floor next to a Barbie the next. There were the horseback riding boots she had to have. I made her pay for half of them. And there are the whines out of their mouths like ``McDonald's again?''—when I recalled that eating out as a child was a big treat.

More than ever, children need to know what it is like to do without. It is a mindset not just a matter of economics. When I look back on how I grew up I now realize that we did not have a lot of money. But I never felt poor. And I always felt an obligation to help others.

I've also tried to make my children more aware of other people in need. We have seen street people in New York City and have been approached by panhandlers at home. Some are needy—some are scamming. We have gone down to the local soup kitchen with some of our money from Christmas presents. And we have collected quarters for the missions. But a part of me worries each day that I must make sure my children realize that the shiny silk threads of life will bring light and catch your eye but it is the coarse regular cloth that holds life together.

Sometimes I will play a ``what if'' game with them. We will be in the car or waiting for a meal in a restaurant and I will ask them what they would do if they won a million dollars. I probably ask that same question about once a year. Their answers have, of course changed. Sometimes they wanted to buy a horse or a farm. Matthew said, one year, that he wanted to buy all the baseball cards in the world. Another time he wanted a toy store and his sister wanted an ice cream shop. Yes, they say that they will save money for college—because that is a big priority in our house. And they say they will give some to charity—I think I have guilted them into that statement. But it is a good exercise because it shows what is important in life and what one would or could do if they had the means.

And you realize that children do not need a lot of things to be happy. They need to experience love and take walks and be read to and share silly times. But a new coat or a big toy will not necessarily make a child happier or better. Sometimes I think it is we adults who worry about giving things to our children. I can remember when Kerry was in first grade she visited a former classmate who had moved to a fancy new home on a large, large lot. I asked her about the house and expected her to compare our place to that. She didn't. I pressed on and asked ``Would you like to live there?'' Now, this house had a grand piano in the living room and space for a lot of other things too. Kerry said casually, ``Not really, their television reception wasn't so good so the cartoons weren't that clear,'' The family had not had cable installed yet so this big home was a bust to my little girl.

I laughed at myself and my own silly worries about what mattered. Kerry just wanted to see her cartoons clearly and be loved. Don't we all.

This year, as an eighth-grader, she was given a writing assignment. She was asked to create a ``basket of memories'' about someone in her life. She chose my father and put some interesting things in her basket.

Throughout the years, my parents had been very generous to the children. They had given Kerry books, toys, jewelry and money. But she did not put in any of those things. Instead, she put in little objects that reminded her of times spent with my Dad. She chose a chicken bone—for the times she went out to eat with my Dad, just her and Grandpa. She chose a paintbrush—for the times he gave her a ride home from art class and they talked and she sang silly songs. She chose a prayer book—because it reminded her of his faith. And she chose a plastic horse—because he had told her stories about when he was in the cavalry in college. Notice that what was important to her was time shared. So if we spend time with our children and those we love we are spending something better and more lasting than money.

REFLECTION

Shiny cars, big houses, name-brand clothes, big vacations, and fancy meals—all of them, from time to time, can be nice. But material things do not make a family better. Nor do they really make one happier. It is good to be secure and have food, clothing and shelter. But happy families, truly happy ones, do not need things. They need each other and a sense of purpose in their life. Help me so I don't dwell on what I don't have. Rather let me focus on what I do have and realize that the really important things in life are not things.

MATERIALISM: SILK THREADS

WEAVING LESSONS

- *Read ``The Emperor's New Clothes'' by Hans Christian Anderson to remind yourself what happens to people who go along with the crowd.*

- *Allowances, savings accounts, little jobs—all of these things will help form a child's view of what life owes him and what he has to earn. Teach a child to work hard and be generous at an early age.*

- *Ask a child to go to their room and make a list of what is a necessity and what is a luxury. It's amazing how many kids think a stereo is a necessity.*

- *Involve your children in some of your spending decisions. Let them know, at an appropriate age, how you have to make choices about what to do with the family income.*

- *Good behavior can be rewarded at times. But don't ever let a child think they are owed a treat or money for doing what is right—like cleaning their room or getting good grades.*

- *Visit a soup kitchen. Or make a meal for the poor and eat the same thing that night for your family. Remind them how those people don't have a choice about what they are going to eat.*

- *Always watch advertisements on television with a critical eye. Say to your kids—do you believe that by wearing that you'll be more attractive or play better?*

- *Remember to enjoy and appreciate the things you do have.*

CHAPTER EIGHT

GROWING PAINS: THE THREADS STRETCH AND TEAR

Families change and grow and develop. New members are added. A bout with chicken pox comes down on a house like a plague. Feelings are hurt and lessons are learned. Sometimes it is through the most difficult times—like a loss of a job—or wonderful times—like the birth of a new child—that families are able to define themselves, and really come together. And sometimes, it is through the most trivial and innocent of hurts or accomplishments, that families can grow too.

No family will exist without pain. People will have bad days at school and work and come home in a bad mood. Children will not be invited to birthday party. Teens will act like adults one second and cry about something the next. There is no perfect family or person. Once people accept that fact then they can weave their family knowing that there will be threads that stretch and tear. But families will be able to patch up the problems, replace the threads and keep working at their life together.

When kids are little, the problems might seem small and even silly but they are very real to them. I remember when Elizabeth was in first grade she came home all excited. "I'm flag person this week," she announced proudly. "Oh does that mean you hold the flag during the pledge of allegiance?" I asked. "No, it means I stand under the flag with my hand over my heart and I lead the class when we say it," she said with a proud and toothless grin.

She was learning to do a job and be a responsible and important part of her classroom life. She was growing up on us and we loved watching her do it. The next week she told us all about the strategies involved with clapping the erasers in the school year. "You have to hold them away from your face," she said in a very serious tone.

Yes, she was growing and learning at age six. But she also learned something the next week that wasn't so nice. She approached me one night and said in a much too casual voice that "maybe I can take the plain, yellow lunch box to school tomorrow." I looked puzzled and asked her why she didn't want her beloved "Barney" lunch box. She enjoyed the big purple dinosaur and had taken it all through kindergarten. I knew she still liked the show on public television. I had even asked her at the start of the school year if she still wanted to take the lunch box and she had said yes without hesitation.

So what brought about this change of heart? I said that she could switch lunchboxes but I gently asked why. It all came out with a few tears. Another little girl at school had looked across the lunch table at her and said "You like Barney?" She said it in a tone that made it sound like only babies could like him and that she couldn't believe anyone would want to carry a lunch box with him on it. Elizabeth told me she didn't respond to the girl. However she came home feeling hurt and confused.

Inside I was laughing a little bit because the lunch box critic wore a Barney rain coat and carried a Barney umbrella all last year. I reminded Elizabeth of this, but I guess that was last year so it didn't count. Kids can be so cruel to each other.

GROWING PAINS: THE THREADS STRETCH AND TEAR

They may feel insecure inside or they may like getting laughs—but for whatever reason—children can hurt each other with words in school.

In a way it was no big deal. My daughter will not be scarred for life over this lunch box incident. But it was an example of problems in family life and how we deal with them.

A part of me wanted to keep Elizabeth home and away from and critical comments or little hurts. Yet, I knew that I could not protect her forever from such pain. But I also realized that I must give her the medicine of confidence and a good sense of self-esteem if she is going to survive. The most important thing about he whole lunchbox business was the realization that home was a place where Elizabeth could share her feelings and find comfort and love. When problems happen at work or school it is good if everyone at home can show support and affection. It a child is cut from a basketball team, it's nice to come home to a hug. If a sale doesn't go through at work, it's nice to feel good at home.

Elizabeth switched lunch boxes the next day. In a way she had outgrown Barney. But I also think she chose to protect herself from the slings and arrows of first grade taunts. A little bit of her innocence was lost through that experience. But I talked with her a lot about doing what she thinks is right and believing in herself. I told her if she wanted to carry a Barney stuffed animal to school it would be fine. She sniffled and felt better. But there probably is still a part of her that wishes she didn't have to worry about her lunch box or hair ribbon or shoes. Still, she knows we care and that we love her.

The pep talks must be working a bit because this year she asked me if she could wear a little cap that had been her grandfather's. It was like an Irish sporting cap. She wore it at an angle and looked adorable. Certainly, I said, you can wear it. Her older brother looked at her and said ``You're not wearing that to school are you?'' She replied firmly that she was. And she did. She wore it for a few days and beamed with pride and confidence. She liked the hat. She liked remembering her grandfather and she liked the way she felt when she wore it. If anyone laughed or noticed—it didn't matter this time.

Now, this doesn't mean that if she chose to pierce her nose I would have patted her on the head and told her it was fine. Home is also where people tell you honestly if you have put on a little weight. And they help you match your shirt and tie. But the important thing is that you know you are loved, even if you need to lose five pounds.

Self-esteem is so critical for a person or a family when trying to deal with problems. Creating a place where everyone feels safe and good is a challenge. It is not easy at school or home.

However, it can be done. I remember when Matthew was younger he came skipping out of kindergarten with two stickers on his tie. He was quite proud of them and seemed to have had a wonderful time at school. I asked him about the stickers and he said he got them for winning at alphabet and number bingo. ``Oh, you mean that two times you were the first person in the class to get bingo?'' I asked. ``Oh, no, he said. ``I was like the ninth or tenth person to call it out. I was the ninth or tenth winner,'' he said with a happy grin.

I couldn't help but smile too. He felt like a winner because his teacher had made them all feel important and successful during that classroom game. He didn't feel sad or upset that someone else had called bingo ahead of him. He was doing his job of learning letters and numbers and getting his stickers—that is what counted.

GROWING PAINS: THE THREADS STRETCH AND TEAR

Many times, when the children come home with little problems at school I find that the best thing I can do is talk it over. If they have made a mistake, we try and learn from it. And if they have been hurt by a nasty comment then all I can do is give them a hug and tell them that I think they are the best. When Kerry was in fifth grade and two girls were giving her a hard time I had her repeat after me ``I am wonderful'' each night. She felt silly and thought I was ridiculous but it worked. The teasing stopped and she knew that there was a safe place for her at home where—no matter what—she would be loved.

Of course there are some pains that are real and physical. The upset stomachs, the early morning fevers and earaches, the chicken pox. Other families have had to face even more serious illnesses like debilitating diseases, or cancer or chronic diseases like diabetes. I have watched my sister-in-law cope with her four-year-old son and his juvenile diabetes.

Having a child with a chronic illness never stops. Things don't get better they just stay stable. It is a day filled with shots and finger pokes and keeping track of foods eaten. It is not the end of the world, but it is difficult.

Certainly there are people who have to cope with far worse things. But when you are watching your little boy and wondering what effect the disease will have—it is scary. Telling him that he is wonderful will help. But there is always that inner fear, that constant worry. The only thing a family can do with something like that is take each day at a time and vow to lead as regular a life as possible. Just remember that no one's life is ``normal'' and that everyone copes with something.

There is, too, the pain that will come with failure. Perhaps a child will do poorly on a test or lose a class election or miss the winning shot in basketball. At those moments nothing quite seems to help. Words sound hollow and the offer of ice cream is small comfort. At those moments you just have to let the child cry it out and sympathize.

I remember when Matthew was in third grade his team lost in a soccer championship by one goal. They might have won except their goalie had to go to a family activity so he missed the game and another player filled in. Matthew played very hard and shook hands with everyone. But when he got in the car the tears came and he was heartbroken. What could I do or say? I told him he had played a great game, and he had. I told him the team did their best under the circumstances, and they had. But mostly he learned what it felt like to lose. It was painful. However, I think that since then it has taught him compassion as his team has beaten other teams. By playing sports for many years he has learned how to lose without as much pain and how to win with a certain amount of grace.

A big part of growing up is owning up to one's responsibilities. I want my children to always tell me the truth but I must be sure that I do not over-react when they tell me something bad. For example, I remember when Kerry told me she thought she had lost her silver charm bracelet. It had been a present for her First Communion so we let her wear it to school the next week as a special treat. At bedtime, I asked her where it was. She said she remembered taking it off for gym class but she couldn't remember seeing it after that. I asked her to try and remember where she had worn it. She said she had worn it at recess in the school parking lot. ``Oh, great'' I thought, "it probably fell down the sewer grate near the gym.''

I was angry at her carelessness but I didn't yell. I thought that she would find the bracelet at school the next day. I told her to go to school and re-trace her steps. "Ask at lost and found and

GROWING PAINS: THE THREADS STRETCH AND TEAR

look carefully in your classroom," I said. When she came out of school the next day, she said she couldn't find it anywhere. We walked around the parking lot and looked for the shiny item—nothing.

It could have been one of those "Why don't you take care of your things?" days. But it wasn't. When she lost the bracelet it reminded me of when I was a freshman in high school. My mother had given me a blue sapphire ring at the start of the school year. It was a family keepsake and she was entrusting it to me at the ripe old age of 13. I took the ring off for gym and didn't put it back on for my next class. Either It fell and was lost or someone stole it. It never showed up at the gym office. Of course, I felt terrible but I remember how my mother didn't make me feel any worse. She was disappointed but she didn't go on about it. Nor did she keep bringing up the ring incident. She recognized I made a mistake and forgave me. So that night I told Kerry how I had lost some jewelry too and that it was okay to make a mistake. She felt better. Happily, for Kerry, there was a happier ending to her story than to mine. She was looking for a bookmark in her room and uncovered the bracelet under a pile of other things. It seems she had worn it home from school but had taken it off quickly so she could go play at a friend's house. Still it was a good lesson for both of us.

There will be growing pains that come from big events in a family. But it is usually the little ones that will determine the way a family will go. If you can cope with spills at the dinner table and lost homework and schedule changes then you can usually rise to the occasion for the big events in a family.

Actually, a lot of times the big events that cause some problems are firsts. They are usually happy occasions but families must make adjustments. The birth of a child, a new home, the start of school, a job change—all of these are stressful but joyful times. Some people cope well with change and adjust easily. Others, like myself, do not.

Each time we had a baby I was so happy. But I also worried if I was going to be a capable and good mother. Our first two children were 17 months apart so even though I worried I didn't have much time to dwell on what kind of job I was doing. I just did it. When Elizabeth was born four years after Matthew I felt overwhelmed but I had the confidence of a third-time Mom. Yet, even though I enjoy motherhood so much there were many days that I cried. Sure part of it was hormones but another part of it was learning to cope and adapt. Fortunately, I was blessed with a husband who reassured me, and parents who helped me.

Families should expect tears and trying times when children join a family. Everyone is tired and hungry and crabby during this experience. But if you accept the idea that family life is trying but beautiful then you can cope.

When we moved to the house we live in right now, I was a mess and there was nothing beautiful in sight. If I looked at things rationally, I would have seen that our new house was just five miles away from our old one and that all would be well. However, I only saw how the children couldn't walk home from school and that we would be away from familiar places. Silly, yes. But my mother was in the hospital at the time and the prognosis for her was not good. I felt that I was losing too much at once. I couldn't change my Mom's condition so I thought that maybe we could just move back to our old neighborhood and be safe. Fortunately, my husband endured my crisis and we learned from it. I, who thought of myself as a strong person, realized how weak I could be. And I realized that one should never underestimate changes in one's

GROWING PAINS: THE THREADS STRETCH AND TEAR

life. The pain I created when we moved showed me how much more I had to grow up. It also left me feeling vulnerable. But it also made me more compassionate, because until that time I had never really felt so confused or hurt.

You must have empathy in a family. You must try and look at a situation through the family members' eyes. For example, the stomach aches and headaches and tears are very real—even if there is nothing physically wrong with a child—when they are about to start a new school year or a new situation. Every August my children have a bit of the jitters. Kerry and Matthew have always headed out the door with a smile on the first day. However, Elizabeth has moved slowly into each new situation. She cried at the start of kindergarten and first grade. Her teachers were lovely and she was prepared academically, but she had watched my parents die within two years of each other and she was close to them. She feared the separation from me and it showed.

It was our job each day to make her want to go to school and to tell her we understood why she was scared or lonely or ready to go home at lunch time. Even this year she will talk about staying home if she has been away from school for a long weekend.

And I must confess it was an adjustment for me to send my last one off to school. I remember when she began I wondered if she would be wandering the playground without a friend. She is shy by nature and a sensitive soul.

Indeed, her older brother reported that he saw her at recess and "she wasn't doing anything." Oh how I wanted to rush over to school and take her hand and introduce her to everyone. I wanted to tell them that she really is funny and delightful and kind-hearted. But I didn't. Because, like the trees in the fall, I had to learn to let go. When a child has a growing pain, sometimes it is necessary to just sit back and tough it out. Certainly you can encourage and hug but there are some things in life that must be learned on one's own.

I listened to Elizabeth tell me how she cried at lunch because she couldn't open her milk carton. I wondered then if I should be a lunch mother every day instead of just once a week. But I knew that wouldn't really help her. It was like teaching a child to walk. You have to let go of the baby's hand and know there might be a few falls or bumps.

And, to be honest, the letting go was hard for me. It was the first time in 12 years that I didn't have a little one with me. I had to learn to function without the sounds of Sesame Street in the morning and the constant companionship of someone else. It was lonely at the beginning and even now there are empty days. Oh I have filled them with more work and activities. And I always manage to have a reason not to do housework. But beginnings and endings are tough and should not be dismissed easily.

When the threads of a family stretch and tear they should not be ignored. And everyone in that family needs to be reminded—during good times and bad—that they are loved and appreciated for who they are. It sounds so simple. But when feelings are hurt and bills need to be paid and everyone is rushing about and late—those simple things can be ignored or forgotten.

REFLECTION

The dog has made a mess on the rug. Your little one didn't get invited to the big birthday party. Your son has a science project due the next day and he has just begun to work on it. The school needs 24 cupcakes. Your mother needs a ride to the doctor. It's raining and you feel as if your world is spinning out of control. As hard as it may sound—take a few seconds to laugh and realize that this is just the ``stuff'' that families are made of. Families are trying and wild and hectic. But take a moment more, and ask if you would trade these precious people for any others. Ask if you could imagine life any other way. And then you should realize that love is not just rainbows and hearts. It is scraped knees and fevers at two in the morning and piano recitals that last for hours.

GROWING PAINS: THE THREADS STRETCH AND TEAR

WEAVING LESSONS

- *During troubled times tell yourself that the sun will come up each day and go down each night no matter what. Resolve to make the most of that time.*

- *Don't be too hard on yourself. So often we worry about things that don't really matter. Will people remember a tense person with a clean house or a welcoming soul that lived in a bit of clutter.*

- *When you are worried ask yourself what is the worst possible thing that could happen. Confront that fear and ask how you would deal with it. Then you will help to control your feelings and your life.*

- *Find time each night to talk a few minutes alone with each child and your spouse. Big problems come when little ones are not resolved. Share your feelings and find out what is happening.*

- *Don't forget to laugh. You can poke fun at yourself and others and shake away those bad moods.*

- *Be honest at home. Make sure everyone feels safe and secure in telling the truth. But if you can truly say what you think and feel then you can talk through tough times.*

- *Prepare yourself when change is coming. Don't underestimate or dismiss the impact it can have on you.*

CHAPTER NINE

DEATH AND DEPARTURES: WHEN THREADS UNRAVEL

The picture of my family a few years ago is quite different than it is now. Then, my children had three grandparents—two nearby and one in Wisconsin. Back then my parents, who lived near us, were at every school and family activity. There were daily phone calls from my mother to inquire about the children's health or day at school, or just to chat. There were visits almost every day by my parents. That was who we were. But that is no more. Both my parents are dead now and it has changed the picture and dynamics of our family. It has been a time of great adjustment.

We are not alone in re-defining who we are and how we live our days. Everyone, at some point experiences the death of a loved one. And, statistics show that many families undergo a different kind of ``death'' with the departure of a parent because of divorce. The faces of families change. The threads unravel and we must begin the weaving process again to make our family into what it wants to be. It is not easy.

There are days when I can't remember what I went into a room to get, but I can recall every moment of the day my mother died. She had several strokes following some elective surgery. She had been in the hospital for a month and was in a nursing home for rehabilitation. She had been there one week but wasn't making much progress. I promised her she would not stay there because I knew that she never wanted to be in a home. I told her we would get her better and get her home. I was telling her my hopes, not reality. She was much too sick and her body could not recover. Elizabeth had just turned four. She and I were with my Dad and we were going to see my Mom that day. I went to see her each day and feed her lunch to her. She had difficulty swallowing and speaking. The home called and said she had been rushed to the hospital.

When we got there we were placed in a private room so the doctors could talk with us. They told us that she had weakened to the point that her body was failing and she wouldn't last a day. I sat there stunned. My brother, sister, father and I cried while my daughter happily colored a picture for her grandmother. None of it seemed real. But it was.

I then went in to see my mother who was breathing into an oxygen mask. She looked so scared and frail. I hugged her and kissed her and prayed with her. But I couldn't say good-bye. I couldn't let go at that point. My head knew that she wouldn't want to live in this weakened condition where she couldn't walk or speak. By my heart kept saying ``I want my Mommy.''

I ran home quickly to meet my husband and make arrangements for the children. I then returned to the hospital—expecting to be there for many hours. However, the nurses told us that she was going quickly. So I ran out to the phone to call my husband and tell him to come and be with me. I confess that I didn't mind the delay at the phone booth. There was a part of me that wouldn't have minded if my mom had died without me being there because I was afraid of death at that moment. Certainly, I had experienced the loss of an aunt and uncle and my grandparents had died. But I had not seen them die—nor had I felt as close to them as I did to my mother.

I returned to the room and stayed with her. My Dad and my siblings were there with her. We held her hand and talked and prayed and kissed her. My godmother—her best friend—started to tell stories about when they were kids. That seemed to lull my mom into a peaceful state. She relaxed and stopped fighting for air. She died peacefully on a Friday afternoon with people she loved.

I can't recall ever hurting so much.

The death of my mother had a profound effect on me and my family. It has taken a long time to recover. My son began third grade after my mom's death. His teacher told me he wrote about wanting her back and wanting me to stop crying. Little Elizabeth started nursery school that year. Her teacher said that sometimes she seemed like a serious, and at times, sad child. Kerry, in fifth grade, had a tough year too. She wanted to stay home a lot more. And my husband, who is so practical, tried to help us focus on the future instead of fretting about the past we could not change. At times I envied and resented his ability to cope. I also admired his generous heart. He welcomed my father to supper almost every night. They talked about work and school and slowly, oh so slowly, we began to heal.

I realized that the death of a loved one is not something we get over. It is something you gets used to. There is a void that cannot be filled. And everyone grieves differently. Just because you do not cry or carry on does not mean that you did not love the person who is gone. And you do not have to be ashamed of your tears either. Sometimes children and adults use anger as an expression for their grief. Matt was mad the nurses at the hospital had not noticed her having the stroke. I found her in the hospital bed—unable to speak.

When my mother died my father was quiet and noble in his sorrow. He prayed, visited the cemetery and talked about living a good life so that he could some day be with my mother.

I found that I constantly wanted to talk about my Mom. It was like keeping her alive to me. However, others could not bear to talk about her. It was too painful.

And my husband, again, came up with an idea. He got a tree for us to plant in our yard. We call it the Grandma tree. The children will sometimes say a prayer near it or wave at it. Elizabeth, in her innocence, will kiss the tree and wave to the sky at her Grandma. All of us are living in sorrow in a different but better way now.

The grieving process is so necessary in a family and must be respected. Families should not pretend things didn't happen. But people shouldn't be forced to talk about their sorrow all of the time.

Time does heal. Time takes away the sting. But scars remain. It reminds me of how I hacked up my fingers with some hedge clippers. The fingers were stitched up and the skin is smooth again. But on certain days, or when I am doing an activity like typing—my fingers ache. They will never be the same—just as families will never be the same after the death of a loved one.

Families will not be worse off—they will just be different. It would be nice to report that after all of the sorrow we experienced with my Mom that life went along smoothly for a while. It didn't. My Dad was diagnosed with cancer just 18 months after my Mom died. And within a year he was gone. In

DEATH AND DEPARTURE: WHEN THREADS UNRAVEL

some respects it was a bit easier because we knew what it was like to lose a loved one. We also had the advantage of knowing that he was definitely going to die so we talked with him and made our peace. We cared for him through a hospice organization and we were able to be with him in his home when he died. Still it hurt.

Again, it has taken time for my family to recover. Those deaths have colored our lives. It has affected my relationships with my siblings and my own family. The children fret a little more when John goes on a business trip. They don't like the separation. And each of them asks me if I am in good health. "Promise me that you will live a long time," asks Elizabeth. I promise her I will. And then I try to turn our eyes on the good things to come and have her look at the future with hope, not anguish.

I am not trying to sweep our grief under the carpet. It is too real. It won't go away like that. But I also realize that eventually families have to go on or be consumed by their sorrow. If you have faith, then you believe in a life after this one. That belief makes peace of mind possible even if you still miss the loved one.

Helping a family through a death is not easy. So often everyone is hurting. Professional help might be necessary. A sympathetic ear is definitely a requirement. The community can help with cards, meals, and compassion.

There are different kinds of losses. I was an adult who lost a parent.

However, I have watched friends cope with the loss of a child. It is an incredible pain. There are no words that can describe it. It shatters one's life and sometimes one's faith. Why? Why? Why? That is what is asked all the time.

There is no easy answer to that kind of sorrow. A planted tree or a sympathy card will not do the trick. That kind of pain takes years and years of work to get through. There is no simple solution or formula. It just hurts. But I know that eventually people get used to life again and that families can survive and even thrive after such sorrow. The human spirit can find something good.

How well I remember the day my father took a turn for the worse. He had received his terminal diagnosis and went on a trip to Seattle with my brother. It was the fulfillment of a dream. However, he returned from the trip so exhausted. He looked terrible as we greeted him at his home. My husband had gone to get him at the airport. My children stared at him in disbelief. They knew then that it would not be long.

John took the kids home and I stayed to help my father bathe and get him comfortable in his hospital bed. It was my sister's night to sleep at the house. I returned home expecting to find emotional children and tears.

Instead, I found happy, eager children who wanted to share some good things with me. The day of my father's return was my son's 11th birthday and the day my daughter, Kerry, became the first female altar server at our parish.

In honor of that occasion, a dear friend had sent Kerry a dozen roses. And my husband had purchased a statue of an angel for her. He also had bought a birthday gift for Matthew and a gift for Elizabeth—just because. They were all excited about their presents and happy to be distracted from their sorrow. The generosity and kindness of my husband and a friend had eased the pain.

DEATH AND DEPARTURE: WHEN THREADS UNRAVEL

So, too, in families this kind of act will always help. Sometimes it won't be appreciated right away—but it will help. Love is never wasted.

This past year, in addition to my personal sorrow, our parish community suffered some great losses. The 37-year-old father of one family in our school and the 33-year-old mother of another family died within two months of each other. A gray cloud hung over everyone. Five children, under the age of seven, were left without a mother or a father.

Matthew, at age 11, looked at me with a challenge in his eyes during all of this. "Okay." he said. "You always say that things happen for a reason. Well why did all of this stuff have to happen? What good could possibly come from those kids losing their parents," he said.

My answer was that I didn't have all of the answers. I told him that in a way some good had come because the whole community had come together to help these families. We talked about how people had put aside their pettiness and problems to make meals, do housework, provide child care and rides. And I added, "You never know, Maybe one of the little boys who lost his mom to breast cancer will go on to find a cure some day because of this. I don't know Matthew why this happened but if you stop believing that there is a reason for everything then nothing will make sense. You have to believe that there is a purpose for even the greatest sorrow."

He nodded, although I don't think he understood all that I was saying. But he did hear me say that everything would be all right. He needed to hear me say that this sorrow had not been a waste. He needed to know that there was a reason or a purpose to life. He needed to see a pattern.

WEAVING A FAMILY

I could have told him how I remember when my uncle died that my aunt was crying in the emergency room. A nearby stabbing victim, with blood on his shirt, ran to a bathroom to get her some toilet paper for her tears.

That same aunt suffered a stroke two weeks later. She spilled her water as she tried to drink it. But then, with the help of a kind nurse, she was able to lift the glass to her mouth and experience the triumph of doing it right. Terrible things happen but sometimes—like after a thunderstorm a rainbow will follow.

So, too, it is with a divorce. Everyone's experience with that is different—just like death. But no matter what the reason or circumstances it hurts. There can be peaceful and amicable divorce agreements and parents can do what is best for the children. But no person who has experienced divorce can say that there was not some pain involved. Children feel abandoned or wonder if they were to blame. Parents are sometimes bitter or left wondering what they could have done differently.

It is sad when a family experiences divorce. But it is not a cause for shame. When a mother or father leaves, the people are still a family. It is just that the threads have unraveled or been readjusted. I have watched friends and family members experience divorce. I cannot speak of it first hand so I won't attempt to provide advice. However, I do know that there is grieving in a divorce just as there is when there is a death. The many feelings cannot be ignored. However, like any pain, it can be endured and one can triumph over the hurts.

Don't be afraid to seek help. You'd go to a dentist if your tooth hurt. Sometimes you have to seek help when your soul hurts. Help might come from a friend, a church, a professional or from reading and journaling. But don't ignore these critical times of death and departure. They must be faced.

REFLECTION

Oh how it hurts when someone dies. A bit of you dies right then and there too. But death, although it will get us all, does not have to have the power to destroy a family. Neither does divorce. Both of these traumatic experiences in a family can be confronted. Help me to see that the past cannot be changed and the future is uncertain. Let death and departure teach me to appreciate today—the now of life. This way I won't waste any more time fretting about things I can't control and I'll enjoy what I have and am today.

DEATH AND DEPARTURE: WHEN THREADS UNRAVEL

WEAVING LESSONS

- *Death and divorce make one feel angry and hurt. It is at these times that people need love the most—even when they say they don't.*

- *Never underestimate the power of a casserole or card. They are quiet reminders that you care.*

- *Do something concrete to help with your grief. Make a photo album. Send a memorial donation to a charity in your loved one's name. Visit with someone who enjoys talking about your lost child or parent.*

- *Don't ignore bad things or pretend they didn't happen. You must go on with your life but you have to talk things out.*

- *Let go of the ``if onlys.'' Don't say if only the doctor had done this, or if only I had been a better wife. They will eat you up. Focus on the ``what now.''*

- *It is true. The glass is either half empty or half full. Choose half full.*

CHAPTER TEN

HAVING FAITH: THE ULTIMATE WEAVER

A ship needs a course for navigation. A driver needs a map. A teacher needs a lesson plan. And a family needs some sort of guiding principle to chart its way. For me it is God. And I believe that for every person a belief in a higher power has to be at the heart of a family. There has to be something beyond ourselves that rules in this universe and makes sense out of chaos.

So much of who we are and what we do as a family will be defined by our beliefs and values. Many educators are now saying that one of the problems in public education is that children are not being taught morals and guiding principles for their lives. Often, they are not being taught at home. The schools are handcuffed because they cannot cross the line into teaching anything that sounds like a religion.

But children need religion. They need to know—this is what our family believes. Perhaps, the family will not attend church all the time. Or, maybe they will not want to belong to organized religion. But there is no getting around the fact that a family needs faith.

What do you say to a little one when their dog or gerbil or Grandpa or baby sister dies? How do you explain such an event? Do you say that the person is in the ground and gone and well—that is the way life goes. Or can you help the child to understand that there is life beyond this one and that a loving God has created this world and will watch over those loved ones in the next.

How can you teach right from wrong in a family unless you have some basic moral belief? Families need to hear that you must not steal. But they need to know the why. They must realize that stealing is wrong because it hurts another human being. For me the Ten Commandments and the Great Commandments of Jesus Christ—Love God with your whole heart and soul and love your neighbor as yourself—sum up the way my family is taking its journey.

Having faith means that you can accept that maybe there is a weaver who knows the pattern of your family better than you do. Having faith means that you realize what matters in life and that you can endure hardships. When my friend had her house for sale she prayed that it would sell quickly. When it didn't, she said that one might think that her prayers weren't answered. ``But maybe they are being answered. Maybe, this is where we are meant to be for now,'' she said with great faith.

When you have faith it gives your family its identity. We pray before meals. We just don't think that the grocery market provided this food or even the hard work of my husband. Rather, we acknowledge that all that we are and eat comes from God.

Having faith means that we begin our car journeys with a little prayer. We ask for God to watch over us and guide us on our trip.

HAVING FAITH: THE ULTIMATE WEAVER

Having faith means that we pay the extra money and send our children to a Catholic school where our faith principles are re-enforced.

Sometimes I am amazed at how much energy people put into their families and parenting. They subscribe to special magazines about raising families. They take great care of their children and rush them to the doctor's office for sniffles and colds. They watch their nutrition and make sure they get their vitamins and eat a well-balanced meal.

Parents hire tutors to help children who are having problems with school. They also enrich the lives of their children with camps and classes and sports. They spend thousands of dollars on computers and clothes for their children.

I truly believe that most parents I have met love their children dearly and try to provide them with the best in life. But so often they neglect the soul of the child. They leave them hungry for meaning in life and naked to face the world as an adult.

These same loving parents either see faith and church as a Sunday morning thing or else they dismiss it altogether. It cannot be. Nothing makes sense unless one believes. Children can choose to reject their faith or even change it when they are older. But it is the obligation of parents to communicate faith and morals to the family.

It is not enough to provide for the physical, educational, and emotional needs of a child. They hunger for a spiritual and moral life. It must be there.

Children are not dumb. There are so many times when they will ask you about deep and important questions in life. If you have a firm belief in your religion then you have most of the answers.

My son, Matthew, is always asking me questions about God and faith. He wanted to know, when he was younger, if there were cheese balls in heaven. Those little orange, crunch balls are one of his favorite snack foods. I told him that I was sure that there was. I wanted him to understand that the afterlife was a place where one felt contented and loved. When he was older I explained that I wasn't sure about the menu but that I did believe in a life after death.

However, as he grew older he wanted to know where heaven was. He was learning about the solar system and couldn't understand where exactly heaven could be. I told him I didn't know. But I had read enough about the teachings of my faith to explain that heaven is more like a state of being than a place. ``They just use pictures of clouds and harps to give you an idea,'' I said. However, I also added that God gives us glimpses of what heaven is like. ``And I know that I have come pretty close to it when I had you and your sisters,'' I said.

Giving your children a good background in faith does not mean that you stop their questioning or thinking. It just means that you guide them in life. "This is what we believe, and I hope you do too," I tell them.

My daughter, Kerry, questioned why she could not be an altar server in our church. I had to tell her that there wasn't a good reason but that we had to accept the rule for now. Happily, when she was 12 the church changed the rule and permitted girl servers. She learned to distinguish between faith and rules.

But rules do go along with religion. I tell my children that they must go to church each week. How can you say you love someone and then not want to be with them I ask. Why would you deprive yourself of the bread of life I also ask.

HAVING FAITH: THE ULTIMATE WEAVER

My mother and father went to church every morning of their lives. They showed me that this is what gave them nourishment. This was how they started their day. This is what was important to them. They did not need to preach to us or make us go to church. We saw the benefits most clearly. Although, in our younger years, my mom did warn us that if we decided we were too sick to go to church we were going to be too sick the rest of the day. We could not go out or ``recover'' for an afternoon of fun.

Children need so much of what religion can provide. When Kerry was 13 she told me she was going to an Eucharistic adoration at our parish. That is when one sits in front of the Eucharist and spends quiet time in prayer. I never thought she would have liked it. But she loved the candles and the shiny gold monstrance that held the Eucharist and the lovely quiet of the church.

We sat together and prayed. She did some spiritual reading and I thought about how wonderful it was that my daughter had journeyed so far in her faith that she wanted to come and be with her God. She may tell me when she is 18 that she wants to join another faith or she may become an agnostic or an atheist. But she will always have the experience of a faith-filled family that may draw her back some day or remind her of what is right.

When I was little my mother used to make us say the rosary on long car trips. I didn't like it. We each recited ten Hail Marys and I was eager for it to be over. For my mom that was a special form of prayer. It was not mine. But I respect that in her and I try to show my children various ways to pray.

When I lifted each of my children out of their cribs each morning I would try and say aloud, ``Thank you God for another day of life.'' I was always aware that there were parents who went to a crib and found their child dead of Sudden Infant Death Syndrome. This little prayer reminded me that I should not take the day or my child for granted. Can you see how prayer and faith influence a family's life?

I must confess that there are not always great moments of prayer in our house or even at church. When the kids were smaller I probably spent more time in church focusing on Golden books, cheerios and a bottle of juice than listening to the readings and sermon. Even when I have quiet time I don't spend it in praise or thanksgiving or meditation. Rather, when I have a quiet moment I make lists about things to do and wonder if I took the meat out of the freezer and when I could deliver the Girl Scout cookies.

A lot of my praying in life has been petition prayer. I have asked God to help me so many times. I have said prayers to find lost pacifiers, library books and car keys. I have pleaded with God to help me get a crying baby back to sleep. And when Elizabeth and Matthew have had surgery for little problems like hernias, I have sought out my God to watch over my beloved children.

I wondered sometimes if I was like a teenager in my relationship to God. Did I only seek him out when I wanted something—like the teen who wants the car or $10 to go to the mall.

But then I realized that God is not like me. He would not be resentful. He told the story of how the vineyard owner paid the same wage to the workers whether they had worked all day or only a few hours. God does not have a scorecard. He is the perfect example of unconditional love.

It is this example that is so important for families because that is what we must be to each other. We must try to be more like

HAVING FAITH: THE ULTIMATE WEAVER

God to each other. I tell my children that they may hurt me and others in the family but I will always love them.

I tell them that families are a safe haven—a place where mistakes can be made. It is my faith that enables me to see what love is really all about. It is my faith that says that there are three things that last—faith, hope and love and the greatest of these is love.

A lot of people are uncomfortable when talking about religion. They think it is not something that one should discuss. I know religious differences have caused division and even war. But when religion takes its proper role in a family, then it can make all the difference between a good family and a great family. It can help you weave a cloth that is warm and secure and close. And even when things unravel or tear it is your faith that helps the mending.

REFLECTION

Christopher Columbus showed those living in fear that the world was not flat. When you live a life of faith you show that the world is a place with a Creator who holds you lovingly in the palm of his hand. You trust that his hand is guiding the weaving of your family. You believe.

Help me to get myself to church and help educate my children about their God. Help me to do what is right in life—even if people think I am a sucker or silly. Help me to pray more and focus on what matters. Help me to give my children the right values so that they may grow to become moral and productive members of our world.

WEAVING LESSONS

- *It is never too early to talk with a child about God. If you do it from the very beginning it will seem natural and the relationship and discussions will grow.*

- *Prayer is powerful and can help heal a family. It also can help them in time of need. And it is a nice way to begin and end your day.*

- *Start by asking you children what they are thankful for each day—that is a prayer. Ask them if there is anything or anyone special they want to mention in their prayers. That, too, is praying.*

- *Subscribe to a newspaper or magazine that focuses on your faith. Display religious pictures in appropriate places to show that you think your faith is important.*

- *Give your children and family the moral guidelines they need for life.*

IN CLOSING...

The weaving of a family is a difficult but wonderful process. Every family's cloth will be different. You might be working with wool and come out with a scruffy and comfortable pattern. Or you might be working with silk and have a delicate and lovely design. Your family might be complicated or simple. It might involve a lot a people or just a few. Take pride in your family. Appreciate its uniqueness. You will have rips and mistakes. You will be different. But with God's help you can weave a family you love. Keep at it and God bless.

To order additional copies of **Weaving A Family**, complete the information below.

Ship to: (please print)

Name _____

Address _____

City, State, Zip _____

Day phone _____

_____ copies of *Weaving A Family* @ $9.50 each $_____

Postage and handling @ $2.50 per book $_____

Massachusetts residents add 5% tax $_____

Total amount enclosed $_____

Make checks payable to *Peggy Weber*

Send to: **Peggy Weber**
81 Stonehill Road • East Longmeadow, MA 01028

To order additional copies of **Weaving A Family**, complete the information below.

Ship to: (please print)

Name _____

Address _____

City, State, Zip _____

Day phone _____

_____ copies of *Weaving A Family* @ $9.50 each $_____

Postage and handling @ $2.50 per book $_____

Massachusetts residents add 5% tax $_____

Total amount enclosed $_____

Make checks payable to *Peggy Weber*

Send to: **Peggy Weber**
81 Stonehill Road • East Longmeadow, MA 01028

Also by William Pauley III

Automated Daydreaming

Hearers of the Constant Hum

The Naked Brunch

The Bedlam Bible

VVLNA (co-authored with Joseph Bouthiette, Jr.)

The Astronaut Dream Book

The Brothers Crunk

The Doom Magnetic! Trilogy

White Fuzz

Nosebleed/Cablejuice

The Mermaid's Gallows

Demolition Ya Ya

If You Don't Sleep, You Don't Dream.

Mr. Malin and the Night.

More Heat Than Light

Goddamn Electric Nights

Spin Doctors Mixtape

Slime Night

The Ballad of Old Joe Booth

Automated Daydreaming

Immerse yourself in madness...

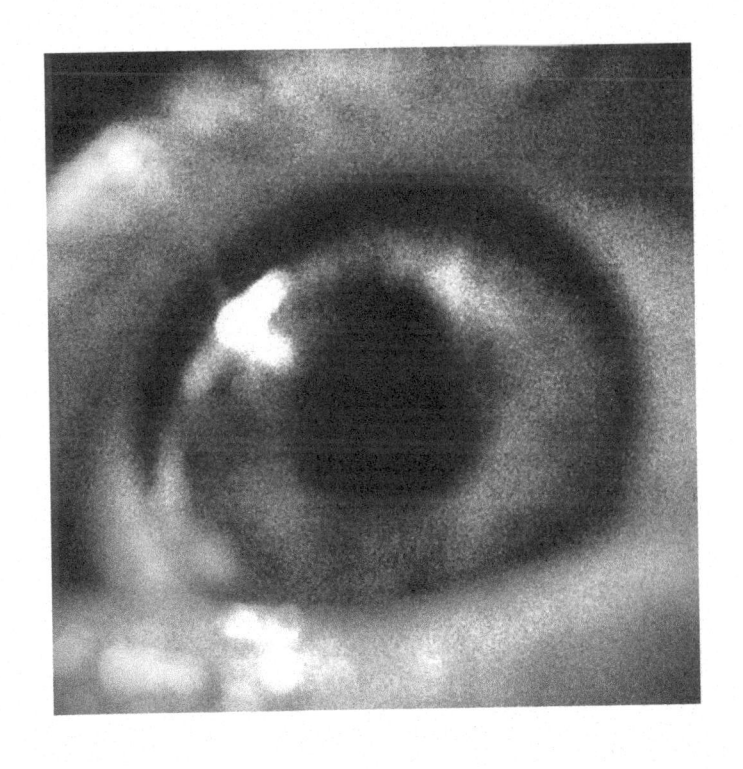

"*You may live to see man-made horrors beyond your comprehension.*"

- Nikola Tesla

POLICE BAFFLED AFTER FINDING REMAINS OF "TELEVISION MAN"

On October 28th, 2015, two Chicago police officers responded to a 911 call concerning a strange smell emanating from an abandoned church. Inside they found human remains, mutilated and wired with electricity, along with evidence supporting the killer was one they'd been hunting for years: Dr Perry Gordon.

Two days later, a letter from Gordon arrived at the police station. He claimed the victim, Airman Bricker Cablejuice, consented to his own mutilation, and that the two were in the midst of a great experiment at the time the police barged in. He also said the victim was still alive, even in his butchered state, and he could prove it. By connecting Bricker's brain into a computer via a surgically installed USB port, the police would be able to download his consciousness and read his thoughts in real time. The contents of the feed, however, would play out in a somewhat distorted and exaggerated manner, due to the brain being in a lucid dreamlike state. In the letter, this process was called 'automated daydreaming.'

Following Gordon's instructions, the officers discovered he was telling the truth. The mangled remains were indeed alive. However, while reviewing the evidence, it was made painfully clear that Gordon's experiment went much further than just physical desecration. If the acts depicted in the feed turn out to be true, it would make Gordon the most heinous criminal the world has ever seen.

But did these monstrous acts of violence even take place? Or was it all just part of the bizarre hallucinatory daydream?

To whom it may concern:

I am not a criminal, nor were my actions inhumane.
    He wanted this. Bricker. He asked for it. I've seen the reports and I've read the articles about him, about me, and they couldn't be more wrong. What they claim as fact is nowhere near truth. Bricker was not taken hostage. He was not held against his will. Again, he asked for this. I was happy to provide this service for him, and that I was *skilled enough* to have been able to provide this service for him. I believe we all have our gifts, something that comes more naturally to us than it does for others, and that gift is what gives us purpose. My gift is helping people, and that was why I felt compelled to offer my services to Bricker. It's as simple as that.
    I think we all know Bricker's gift by now, as the media has covered it extensively in the last forty-eight hours (and years ago, after falling from the plane, if you are able to remember that far back). It's been two full days since police found "his remains," at least that's how it's being worded in the reports. What they found are *not* remains, well at least not in the way they're making it seem. The random bits of his corpse, a bucket of entrails, the brain in

a jar—those are not *pieces* of him. They are not his "remains." What I mean to say is that what they found is *all of him*. Every bit. He is complete, and absolutely *alive*. I understand the confusion, why he was reported dead, and even the reasoning behind ordering a manhunt for his "murderer," *for me*. I mean, to the untrained eye, he certainly *appears* to be dead, but that brain is more conscious and more aware than yours, or even mine. You see, Bricker is living in the *multiverse*.

Let me back up for a moment. I'm getting ahead of myself.

Everything alive on this planet exists in its current form thanks to mutations, and nearly 4 billion years of mutations at that. Mutations have made us more efficient in the ways of survival. Despite having only been on earth for something like two-hundred thousand years, humans have quickly climbed to the top of the food chain. Here, in present day, we are the most efficient and intelligent beings in the entire universe, as far as we know. We've never seen any creature greater than humans in our current form.

Until now, that is. *Bricker*. He is a superior species. Our evolution. He's what's next.

Through a wonderfully bizarre mutation, *immortality*, Bricker has been naturally selected to populate the earth with the *post-human*. In his long life, he will have mated with countless women, most of which will all have children carrying his mutated gene and hopefully have Bricker's exact traits. Now, I'm sure this question will come up at some point, so I will go ahead and answer it now: *yes*, I did approach his children, those who are now adults anyway, and they all refused my offer to study them, as I have their father, and I have respected those wishes. *Honored them.* I am not a monster. I am a man of science. Had Bricker refused me, I would have respectfully walked away and left him to his life. But Bricker didn't refuse. He wanted this. He needed me to show him why his gift was important, why he was special. He looked at it as a burden before I came into his life. He was severely depressed and found no meaning to his existence. He asked me to give him purpose, so I did. The media is making it out to be something it isn't, however. We had an agreement, a respect for one another, and most importantly, an understanding of how important our research was.

We were changing the world before the police barged in and confiscated my equipment, and Bricker. They aren't even concerned with our research, at least from what I can tell through reports. They are only interested in finding me. They want to put me to death for a crime I did not commit. They want to lynch me for bettering the world, our species and the future species, and for my many contributions to science. That doesn't seem like justice, especially when the supposed deceased is not even deceased.

Which brings me to the purpose of this open letter. I am not interested in clearing my name, well, at least not primarily. It would be nice not to be hunted, but I'll deal. My fate is not the most important factor here. The work is what is important. The research. I am writing so that you do not discard of Bricker. Do not bury or do whatever it is police do with what they think are human "remains." I am not concerned the burial will kill him, cause as I said before, he is immortal. Do with him what you will, but you know just as well as I that it's just not good etiquette to bury or discard living things. It's not right, and Bricker certainly deserves better. Despite your coroner's observations, he is alive...and I can prove it.

To anyone with access to the things confiscated from my lab (I'm presuming all of it is now labeled with the word 'evidence'):

retrieve the red notebook and turn to the page that has the words 'automated daydreaming' written across the top. It should be about two-thirds of the way into the notebook, and if memory serves me, the entire page is written in purple ink. This page contains instructions on how to download Bricker's consciousness onto any machine containing an accessible USB port. It is a live feed of his thoughts, as again, he is alive, and the information comes quick in spurts of text, so it is probably beneficial to let it run for about an hour or so in order to get a good chunk of reading material. Just a warning though, if you let the feed run for anything longer than an hour, you will see that the information loops, and you'll also notice that when it does, some of the information changes. This is normal. Bricker's mind is more complex than the human mind, as we currently know it. As I mentioned before, he is living in the *multiverse*. This is completely due to my actions, as I introduced certain machinery into his system that triggered this response. He agreed to all of it, of course. Sorry if it feels like I am repeating myself. I want it to be absolutely clear that I had Bricker's consent.

    Before ever knowing Bricker, I was working hard on creating this device to provide evidence to help support the *many worlds theory*, the idea that we all exist in perhaps an infinite amount of universes, or dimensions, all at the exact same time as what we perceive to be our primary existence. In each of these dimensions, we all exist in an infinite amount of ways, doing everything and being every type of person possible. Quite literally, in theory, we all exist in every way possible, have been everything, have seen everything, and have said, touched, tasted everyone and everything in existence. My device only explores five of these worlds (possibilities), or channels, as I prefer to call them. The live feed you'll download of Bricker's consciousness will have explored each of those channels, and may switch back and forth through each, seemingly at random. Bricker controls this.

    Oh, and you should also be warned that as time goes on, each of the channels typically become even more outrageous and outlandish than the ones that came before it, before each loop cycle resets, that is. I know, it's a lot to take in. It may not make complete sense to you now, but once you read the text from the live feed, I assure you all of this will process a bit more smoothly. I should also add that in all the years I've spent analyzing this data, I've found that the facts and specific details of major moments in Bricker's life are still present, however at times it can seem somewhat distorted. Everything that ever meant anything to him in life, that is to say his life in his *present* universe, is buried deep within the bones, inside the structure of the stories of each of the lives looping continuously within the realms of each channel. You'll have to sort through the fiction to find the facts, but I promise you it's all there somewhere, so *pay attention.*

Good luck.

Oh, and I'd appreciate it if this letter and the 'automated daydreaming' feed were published as proof of my innocence, and to set the record straight with the public that Bricker Cablejuice was not murdered, he is in fact alive and well, and functioning better than ever, paving the way for our inevitable post-human society. This isn't necessary, of course, and I'm honestly not even expecting anyone to do so, but it would be helpful, to both me and anyone working within the field of science.

This study is important. The results should be analyzed and used as a stepping-stone for the eventual release of consciousness from the prison that is the human brain. One small step for man, one giant leap away from mankind. *That's catchy, huh?*

However, again, the important thing here is to realize that Bricker is still alive, and

should be treated as every other living being, if not better. He is the key to the future of mankind, in whichever shape or form that may take, and his importance should never be reduced to anything less.
Thank you for your time.

Signed,

Dr. Perry Gordon
Formerly of URIK Labs

c:/automated_daydreaming.exe

[41] NOSEBLEED/ CABLEJUICE

- Part One -

I remember the nausea, then everything went black.

There wasn't a memory for days after that [maybe there was, but I certainly have no recollection of it now]. All I remember is the heavy feeling in my gut as I stared down at the world [thousands of feet] below me, little houses on the hill all looked like little pills to me, and the guy behind me pushing against my back. I was the only thing standing between him and the all-American feeling of freedom. Freedom in the form of nothing, in a swallow, in a fall.

I'll be the first to admit, I was frightened. Days before the jump we were all men—red meat eating, fist pounding, beer guzzling men [we fucked our wives and came on their naked breasts every night a game wasn't on, as man as it gets, by god]—but in that moment, standing up there in the clouds [where man was never intended to be] and looking down at the expanse of civilization below us, and realizing in that moment too that mankind are no more than insects [looking down at our anthills from the view of God's eye was when I first felt the nausea swirl inside my stomach], we were not men, we were drones, robots, followers of the machine. Standing there on the edge of the plane, as I was trying to get myself to man up and jump, my knees buckled, I tensed up, and lost all memory of everything I had ever known.

In an instant, I was nothing.

In the next instant, I was falling.

Someone pushed me. Someone behind me on the plane, another soldier [one that was either more man than me for his bravery, or less man than me for his ignorance], grabbed me by the pack and shoved me out the back hatch with all his might. I was falling. I knew I was falling, but I felt nothing. I knew how fast I was traveling, my body knew the precise moment to expect full on collision with the earth below, but my mind was wiped, tired, and traumatized. I could not get my hands to pull the parachute release, to save my own life—as much as I tried, I could not think of a single reason to do so.

I continued to fall long after the other soldiers' chutes had all blossomed. The farther I fell, the faster I fell. My body became hard like steel, like an atom bomb dropped from a plane. In that moment I was atomic, delivering my own personal doomsday.

I was a shell.

I was delivering the weakest message from God to the people of earth.

I was absolutely nothing.

The minute it took my body to jump from the plane to collide with the earth felt more like hours, days maybe. I thought of everything and nothing all at once. I was scared, I was brave, I was something otherworldly.

When I hit the ground, it hurt, but not like it should have. In reality, my ass and my boots should have both met the ground by passing through my flattened skull, but it didn't happen that way at all. In fact, all I felt that day was a little pressure on my face, enough to break the cartilage in my nose and cause a little bleeding. My face hit first, buried itself a few inches in the ground [I landed out in the dry cracked desert], and my body followed as it skidded out about one hundred feet.

Then my legs, which were hanging over my skull like wicked tree limbs, finally fell to the ground. A cloud of dust engulfed me.

I wish I had a better explanation for it—something interesting, something provocative, something that would help answer the many questions everyone had for me afterwards—how I can fall from a plane, speeding through the clouds, for thousands of feet, crashing into the earth at God knows what speed, and come out with only a nosebleed—but I have nothing.

I've only recently remembered these details. It's been something like two months since the fall and this is all that's come back to me. Maybe something will happen, like a dream or a stumble [if I hit my head against something hard, then surely I will remember, as it always seems to work in the movies], and suddenly I will remember everything.

Until then, there is only this.

I am Bricker Cablejuice, the human glitch.

I wasn't sure why this memory was always the beginning of the cycle, as it was a memory from many years ago, and so far back in my past that it didn't make any sense for it to be placed before the memory that always played out next. Where were all the other memories, the ones from the years between? I deduced that this first memory came from the year 1949, given the event took place during my stint in the military [I was honorably discharged almost as quickly as I was enlisted, after falling from the plane, understandably]. The memory that immediately followed was a memory occurring many decades later. Fifteen to be exact...

CHANNEL//FORTY-ONE

When I looked out the window this morning I saw an old man sitting down at the bus stop. When I say old man, I mean a man of the age of eighty. When a man is eighty, he feels eighty. He's an old man, no two ways about it. Bones become weak and frail, legs walk slower, mouth talks slower, lungs breathe slower. Everything becomes difficult. Even the easy things in life, like checking the mailbox, become difficult, some days even impossible. A man longs for death at that age, and the only good thing about it is that he's nearly there, it's within reach. Men are crumbling ogres at the age of eighty. I should know, I've been eighty twice already.

It took me an hour to get from my bed to the window. Getting to the window from my bed in a single hour is major progress for me. Seems I've mastered the system. I have pushed myself to the limit and now can fill my day with twice as many activities as before. Filling my day with activities has only recently become a concern of mine. Before, I used to lay in bed most of the day, not even getting up to shit or piss. I'd let the nurses worry about it. I used to laugh about how long those gals had to attend college, how hard they'd have to work, just so they could wipe up someone else's shit. They're all glorified janitors, babysitters. I don't laugh about it anymore though. Life, for those people, is so short. Wasted time in a life that short is the greatest shame. Wasted time for a man my age, a man of one hundred and sixty-three, seems like it'd feel the same as fifty-pound weights around the ankle of an eagle, so I can't imagine how it must feel for normal folk.

I'm not saying I'm not guilty of it too, cause I am, and I'll be the first to admit it. Like I said before, I've wasted quite a bit of my life, nearly all of it, to be completely honest. I've taken my life for granted time and time again, and I've even spent a good portion of it trying to end it. My body has been abused in ways that would have killed other men, and I have the scars to prove it. I used to think this body of mine was a curse, but now I know it's more than that. I kick myself when I think of all those years I spent lying in bed, depressed as all hell, wishing I was just like those other folk, normal folk. Surely I was put here for a purpose. Surely God had a reason for me.

Okay, I'd like to keep this here confession honest, so to do that, I have to admit now that I really never have been much of a religious man. I'm not entirely sure what I believed in before, if anything at all, but if I dig real deep I can say that I most likely always knew that there was something more to life than just living, fucking, and dying. There had to be. Even before I ever suspected my immortality [or what I assumed was immortality. I was getting older, my body was aging, I was an eroding collection of bones in a thin skin sack, but I would not, could not, die. Or at least I hadn't...yet], I had an undeniable feeling of a consciousness living somewhere within the air that surrounded me, what I assumed was the presence of a higher being. But what was that higher being and how did it relate to me and my role in the world? I had this and countless other questions in my mind, always, even now, only now I'm not too afraid to dive into the unknown, just too old.

This reminds me, I was a scared child. Everything from shadows to water, I feared it all. I used to be convinced that the devil lived inside my earhole [I swear to God I could hear the demon banging on my eardrum every single goddamn electric night]. I can't say it was the devil for sure, but *something* was in there. Something *unnatural*. Maybe even *supernatural*. I used to try to drive the little bastard out, weird things like sticking the sharp-end of a pencil inside my ear, piercing the eardrum, or years later pushing a lit cigarette into it, scorching my ear flesh. Ended up causing permanent damage to my hearing [even to this day, in my left ear, the world still sounds like the inside of a seashell to me].

Bricker, the demon used to say to me, *Bricker you're a goddamn wolverine. You can't teach your tricks to anyone. No, son, you were born with it. You're a goddamn wolfcat.*

I never felt like the demon really ever knew me at all. Of all the years, of all the tragedies, of all the triumphs, I thought that damn demon would have figured me out a little better than it had. It never felt real to me. At least that's what xxxxxx tried to get me to believe [I don't have a single thing to say about that man. I refuse to speak about my encounters with Him. The man was a tyrant and I wasted a good portion of my life pouring out to Him. I will not spend any more time speaking His name and retelling His teachings. I won't have it].

I did, however, find it strange to be staring down at a man, half my age, that caught my eye initially because of his striking resemblance to xxxxxx. Could He have had a younger brother? It seemed impossible given all I knew about the man, or at least very unlikely. Although I never saw xxxxxx as an old man [His appearance when I last saw Him was that of most fifty-year-olds] I was certain that this man, the one I was staring down at through this nursing home window, could not have been Him. xxxxxx would have to have been much older than this man. xxxxxx would have surely been dead by now. No way in all of Hell that the man on the street was one in the same. In all of Hell. No way.

I stood in the window most of the day. The man never moved from his place on the bench. Buses came and went, but the man did not budge from his position. I was convinced this was not Him, however, I did not look away from him, even for a second, the entire day.

Only once did he move. Once. For a while I was convinced he had sat on that bench and died there, perhaps frozen to death, or maybe his heart had given out, I thought, but I was proven wrong the moment he moved.

Yes, he moved.

He looked up at me. He raised his head and looked straight at me as I stood in the window staring down at him. He didn't look around. He didn't catch a glimpse of me out of the corner of his eye. He looked directly at me. There was no emotion shown on the man's face, not from what I could tell anyway [my eyesight is terrible, exactly what you might imagine from eyes as old as these]. I could definitely see the shadows that hung over his eyes and across his cheeks though, and behind the shadows, although blurry, those eyes, the whites of his eyes burned images into mine, specters, ghosts, they were all there, as they always were in xxxxxx.

His stare made me remember things and forget them again, all within seconds. So many images, memories, reveries danced before my retinas. Then they were gone.

And that was all. That was all he did from that moment on, stare. I did not turn away. Invisible ropes of tension wrapped themselves tightly around our eyeballs, and our stares dared the other to walk across the line, into the unknown.

At this moment I knew it was xxxxxx. Had to be.

Then, for no reason at all, I fell asleep. I wasn't even tired; in fact, as I mentioned earlier, I had just woken up an hour before. My eyelids grew heavy and I fell into unconsciousness all within a fraction of a second. Clouds of darkness swirled around the room, opened its hot mouth, and took me inside it.

The world would appear much different to me the moment I'd awaken.

That night I dreamt about honeybees. In the dream, the bees were all disappearing, fleeing from their hives all at once, overnight. Complete and total abandonment. The only bees that remained were the queen and the many younglings. No telling where the others had gone.

But I knew.

I knew because I had been to this place before, the place of erasure, of erased things. Colony collapse disorder, that's what they called it. For one reason or another, an entire colony would vanish. I thought about this as I slept, what it meant to completely disappear from the world and how something could leave everything it's ever known, the only place it ever called home, for emptiness, for darkness, for complete nothingness. I couldn't relate to the idea myself, but it made me dream of other humans and what would happen to them if they all had suddenly disappeared, vanished, without a trace. Gone. I suspected it would have been much quieter, peaceful, that is, given what was left roaming this god-forsaken planet wasn't worse than humans themselves. There are worse things than humans, after all, much worse. I had seen them, and unbeknownst to me at the time, I'd be seeing them again, there in that very dream, or what seemed like a dream to me then.

Soon I'd be seeing everything again. Everything I'd ever done—all the good, all the bad—would soon be playing back to me [some of the sins were unspeakably horrid, but I am nothing if not honest. No matter how terrible a person this makes me out to be—it's the truth]. Memories arrived in the form of ghosts, and they vanished as quickly as they appeared.

CHANNEL//THIRTY-TWO

A memory swirled...

I was standing in a familiar room. It was dark and I was a much younger man then. I removed a handgun from the holster at my ribcage; the leather shoulder straps were the only item I was wearing on this particular night. Standing naked in the living room of my home, what once was my family's home [they had long since left me alone], I held the gun nervously, with copious amounts of stress raking at the tendons of my trigger finger in short, quick spasms. There were pictures staring at me in all directions, the smiling face of my daughter, my wife…my son, my little boy's eyes were looking straight at me. Goddamn it, if I knew that day was going to be the last day I would ever see him, things would have been different. I would have been a better father to him, I would have been there every second. I wouldn't have wasted so much goddamn time doing other things, pointless things that meant nothing. I would have been better.

But he was gone, and my wife and daughter were gone too.

I was a man, alone, and being alone meant drinking whiskey straight from the bottle and fingering the trigger of a gun. Without families, men teeter over the line of being dangerous to themselves and being dangerous to others. Some men even find themselves on both sides of that line.

There was heavy rain that night with mighty winds that rattled the windows and shook the doors, as if the storm itself were desperately seeking shelter, a way inside, protection from the horrors of itself, and in that way the storm and I were one in the same. The rain fell hard against the roof and collected in giant puddles out in the yard, nearly flooded completely. The rain reminded me of a time I would've much rather forgotten, the time we [my family and I] headed to the coast. For most, visions of the beach and family vacations were sweet memories, something cherished. For me it was the physical manifestation of the darkest reservoirs of my mind, an actual place of fear. No man should ever have to feel the pain I've felt there in that place, on that dark coastline.

Images, haunting photographs, of my family, of my son, my little boy, flickered behind my eyelids like a horror film in a cold, empty theater. The gun in my palm suddenly felt as if it were holding me, and not the other way around. I felt as if the house was holding me hostage instead of protecting me from the storm. Everything around me felt like a trap. I was feeling paranoid and strangely claustrophobic and everything felt insane to me, unreal and cold. Unreasonably [I know that now], I felt the gun could cure these feelings, the uncomfortable sensation of strangulation.

Turns out, I was wrong, but damn if I didn't try.

When I opened my eyes, I noticed shadows dancing on the ceiling, watching as I unloaded two bullets into my temple with the only injury being a slight headache. They were taunting me, taking shape of my every failure. I couldn't even kill myself. Even the biggest failures still succeeded at suicide, so where did that leave me? What was I now?

In that moment, I wanted to cry. I *needed* to cry, but the tears would not form. Sometimes it's necessary to let emotions destroy you, to let go, to lose total control of yourself. I could not. I stood there, shaking, nervous, frightened, all under stares from the countless photographs hanging in frames on the walls. It was out of utter frustration that I shot at the ceiling. Four bullets left the chamber of my gun and pierced clear through the roof directly above my head. Rainwater leaked in through the bullet holes, four constant streams pouring down upon the crown of my head. The water was cold and uncomfortable, but also somehow soothing. It was nice to feel something different for a change, even if it was unpleasant.

The gun I was holding would not kill me, I knew that even before shooting myself with it, as I had played out various versions of this night many times before. I wanted nothing more than to die, but nothing would end me, the gun would not fucking kill me.

I could kill others with it, I suppose, but the only man I wished to kill [the man who murdered my son, my little boy] may as well have been a ghost. He didn't seem to exist. All I knew was my son was with me one moment and the next he was gone. Hours later he was dead, murdered, but without a murderer. The cops found nothing, no sort of clue, no finger pointing in any direction at all. They shrugged their shoulders, told us they did the best they could, then gave up, leaving me and my wife and our daughter alone, knowing that our son's killer was somewhere out there in the same goddamn world we were living in. Everyone became a suspect to me, to my wife. We were forced to live a life of unhappiness, to never trust another human being as long as we lived. We got so caught up in it, in fact, that we turned against each other. We began blaming one another for our unhappiness and lost the only thing either of us had left. My wife and

daughter, they left me, here in this very room, years ago. I've been trying to end the nightmare ever since. But this gun would not kill me. Nothing would. Goddamned curse.
 I'd be forever Adam.

Static swirled behind my eyelids and soon other visions would appear to me...

CHANNEL//FORTY-ONE

I was hoping there would be a way around it, a way I could share with you my story and not have to mention xxxxxx or His experiments, but I'm struggling. I'm finding that I am wasting more of my precious time [time has never been more sacred to me than it has in the past day, with the old man sitting outside my window, ghosts in his eyes and his constant staring. I can't even gaze upon him now without falling into tiny comas] trying to find a way to avoid the man than if I were to just clench my jaw and let His ideas flow, in the form of words, or perhaps a beam of light, carrying my thoughts directly into your skull. I apologize for the information you're about to sew into your mind. You will never be able to un-learn this, it will forever be a part of you. It is for this reason alone I feel the need to apologize. And even that doesn't seem like enough, but it's all this tired old soul can offer at the moment.

It wasn't long after I had fallen from the plane when I had first come in contact with xxxxxx. I suppose I was sort of a celebrity at the time, the media went wild over me. The world couldn't get enough of my story. I was featured in all the big publications and even made a couple appearances on television, which was a big deal at the time. I was looked at as some sort of hero, but not the type I would have been proud to have been. No, instead I was looked at as some sort of *superhero*, some kind of immortal freak.

"*Airman Bricker Cablejuice: World's Greatest Anomaly,*" I remember one of the headlines read. Another was, "*Doctors Call Cablejuice a Human Glitch.*"

At first I felt adoration from all the attention, but that quickly faded as I soon became known as an error, an inexplicable mutant. I became incredibly depressed and refused to make any further public appearances or keep any appointments with the media. It was right around this time that xxxxxx found me.

    To truly understand my state of mind during that time, and why I would have ever agreed to work with xxxxxx in the first place, I'd imagine you'd have to have actually been there, standing in my very boots, having the world come down on you the way it came down on me. I became fragile. The only man in history to have ever survived free falling from such an incredible height [and escaping death with only a nosebleed] and there I stood, fragile. My body was untouchable, my spirit was shattered. Again, I was a shell. Atomic, but defused. He showed up at precisely the right moment, as if He were lurking somewhere in the shadows around me, waiting for this moment to arrive. I desperately needed to believe in something, as I was discovering in those moments too that suicide was not an option for me [blood loss only made me nauseous]. xxxxxx gave me something to believe in, for a while anyway.

He knocked on my door and I answered. He stood tall, taller than me, draped in a grey trench coat and black wide-brimmed fedora. He was carrying a black briefcase in His hand. He introduced Himself to me and asked if He could come inside. I nodded and shut the door behind Him.

"You are a gifted man," xxxxxx said to me, "God has put you here for a reason."

"I am cursed," I said.

He sat on the sofa and removed something from His briefcase. It looked to be some sort of electronic dial.

"Not a curse—a wonder, a miracle," He said. "You are exactly what I need. God does answer prayers."

He handed the dial to me. There were several wires sprouting from the back of it. It was black with tiny white numbers printed around it: 41, 32, 23, 14, 5. As I examined it, He told me it would be a part of me, that I was the only one alive who could survive the procedure.

"What procedure?" I asked.

He looked up at me with wet wild eyes, seemingly swirling with blue flame.

"You are to become something of a hybrid," He explained. "Through careful installation of machine parts into your body, you will gain access to a variety of consciousnesses."

He paused and pointed at the dial held in my hands.

"This dial will allow you to...switch channels, if you will, flipping back and forth between consciousnesses, living lives of many different people all at the same time. Like some sort of...*television man*, I suppose."

What He was saying didn't make much sense to me. Television itself was fairly new at the time, and somewhat magical to those of us who didn't understand the technology side of it, so the thought of the machine being inside me, an actual part of me, was completely unfathomable. However, given my fragile and somewhat broken state of mind, I found the idea of being able to run from one life to another rather alluring.

It didn't take much thought before I accepted His offer and agreed to go through with the many procedures. After all, I was suicidal, and the worst that could possibly happen was that I would die, finally be allowed to die. I had nothing to lose and many lives [many escapes] to gain. However, I was foolish. There were worse consequences than death, I would find. Soon, I'd have five different lives, all of them lonely, all of them terrifying in one way or another. And worst of all, I was forced to live all five of these lives forever, until the end of time. Until my last breath, whenever/if ever that would happen.

The first operation transpired that night, the installation of the dial into my skull. He did it right there in the living room of my home, without anesthesia or proper surgical tools. Before the operation, He asked me for a steak knife, a claw hammer, and a handful of rags. As far as I knew, these were the only tools He used to wire the dial into my brain. He said it was the riskiest of all the operations that lay ahead of us, that all the other components relied on the success of this one particular procedure.

And it worked. Afterwards, I felt a new sense of being. I felt important. I felt as if I were contributing to knowledge, to science. I felt like a *future man*. And it brought me closer to God. There was finally a purpose for me, I thought, a reason to live, a meaning behind my freakish gift. I finally knew why I was placed here on this earth. It all made sense to me, and all this was realized within those precious moments.

But as the operations continued, as I became increasingly less human, God would prove to be the furthest thing from me.

CHANNEL//TWENTY-THREE

Static. Static. Static. Static. Stat—

The room was always cold, as if the doctors were trying to keep us cancer patients from rotting, stinking up the place. Chemotherapy felt a lot like a nursing home for smokers in that we all had lived our lives sucking the cancer from tobacco sticks [our lips wrinkled in long thin lines, our mouths looking somewhat like an eyeball with ugly spider leg lashes stretching from our lips across our even uglier faces] and had in a way graduated to this, our final place of rest and the last stop on the long road of life. I'm a tired woman. I've been around so long, I'm ready to go. Don't be sad for me. *Ha! Like anyone would be!* Some become genuinely depressed when they're told they have cancer and that treatment must begin immediately in order to have any real chance of survival, others *love* it. Some of us have waited for this moment all our lives. Cancer was the ultimate pity. No matter how shitty a person I'd been in my life, no matter how many birthdays I missed, people I hurt, money I owed, all would be forgiven when this one word was uttered: *cancer*. It was a godsend.

Of course, the only ones happy to hear the news are just that, shitty people. Those of us who have led shitty lives and have been generally shitty to everyone who had ever cared for us, we're the ones reveling at the thought of having a disease writhing around within us, eating away until there's nothing left. And not only did we have *a* disease, we had *the* disease, *the* cancer. This was the biggest disease there was, the most famous, or infamous, rather. There's no need explaining a thing like cancer. The word speaks for itself. I for one had never felt better than the day I was officially diagnosed. It wasn't long after I abandoned my family, leaving my parents' house one night to go out with a girl I had just met hours before. I like to think of her as my true love, but I guess we didn't know each other well enough to really know for sure. She was the only girl I ever loved. Hell, she was the only *person* I ever truly loved, be it man or woman. We drove out to the coast that night, without a care in the world. Just the two of us. The memory made me smile just as much as it made me wish for death. Thinking of that girl was goddamn bittersweet.

Oh, Haley. I'm so sorry...

Anyway, I returned home, grew up to be nobody, and not a single soul ever gave a legitimate shit about me. Not a one. And that's with a husband, three children, and seven grandchildren, and hell, there were even great grandchildren and great, great grandchildren thrown in the mix too. I couldn't keep up with them all. None of the little shits cared one bit about me! But, hell, if I was being honest, I'd have to say a lot of it was my fault. I'd been put through life's ringer, spit out on the other side, and lived to tell the tale. Wish I hadn't. *Oh, lord, how I wish I hadn't!* There was so much guilt festering inside me I could feel it corroding around my bones, and living with that kind of guilt leads to madness. See, the thing with Haley happened so long ago that anyone who even knew her would be long gone by now, I realized that decades ago, but still it eats at me, even worse than this cancer. *And the mermaids. All those beautiful mermaids...*

So, yes, it was my fault my family didn't love me, but with my disease, I was holding the key, the key to getting my life straightened out, the key to forgiveness, and the ultimate weapon—pity. I finally had an A-list disease, and it was about damn time too. I was getting mighty tired of living. They say life is short, but once you make it to the triple digits, you feel like begging whatever god exists above to be taken out back and put out of your misery with a shotgun blast to the face. If that would have worked for me, I damn sure would have tried it. Maybe not when I was younger, back when I was such a goddamn coward, but after the incident with the mermaids, surely.

I have to stop thinking about this.

After the diagnosis, I immediately called everyone I knew, my children first. It was the first time I had called them in over twenty years. I didn't even recognize my daughter's voice when she answered the phone. She cried at the sound of mine. Twenty years of absence, silence, pure abandonment on my part, forgiven after I uttered that one beautiful word: *cancer*. She must have silently notified her brothers, my two sons, because not long after I uttered the word they had joined in on our conversation, calling in from their own phones. They sounded scared, as if horrified at the idea of losing the mother they never really had in the first place. I imagined them sitting somewhere in their houses, perhaps in complete darkness, holding their loved ones and weeping at the thought of my disease-ridden body. As if bringing their lives into this world somehow made them want to forgive me, despite all my shameful actions, as if they were willing to accept any excuse in order to forgive. Now they had it, and all those years wasted on neglect would have to be made up within the short time frame I had left. That was exciting for them, but only because they didn't know what I knew. They thought I'd die in a brutally violent way, with the disease filling every empty pocket within my body and savagely eating away at me until I had nothing left, but I knew better. The cancer would not kill me, only punish me further, and I was ready. *Good god, did I deserve such a punishment!* The sins I committed in my time were so horrid, I came to expect the worst kind of fate, and I accepted my disease with open arms. I was secretly hoping after our conversation was over, after my children had hung up their phones, that they were sitting there in complete silence, blaming themselves for my disease.

Before the cancer came along, I often wondered what my children were doing, what their lives had grown to be in our time apart. I wasn't even sure any of them were still alive before the cancer brought us back together. I wondered, but not enough to actually make the call to find out. Looking back, I'm not sure if it was because I was scared, ashamed of myself, or if I truly just did not care enough to know. It wasn't until after the cancer conversation, after I was sitting in the cold chemotherapy room [a room that housed only strangers to me] with not a single familiar soul at my side, that I realized in all that time on the phone with each of them, I hadn't even asked how they had been these last couple decades. They asked me about everything. They wanted to know every last detail of my life they'd missed. Hours of conversation, all about me. I thought about calling again, this time focusing one-hundred percent on them, but just the thought of it made me anxious. I would not call them back, not until the cancer spread even further and I had something more to say, to report. *Jesus.* Even I realized how unbearable I was just thinking that. I couldn't even fake showing interest in my own goddamn children's lives.

All I could manage to do was imagine the disease growing inside my body, eating away at internal tissues the way a vulture picks apart the dead. I wondered how advanced it would get, considering my body and the way it never seemed to give up [I should have died many, many times before, with all my…*experiences*], it would never die. *How far would the cancer spread?* I once dreamed the disease took over the majority of my body, and I suffered there on a hospital bed with my extremities gone, decomposed, left with only a rotting brain, two blind eyeballs, and a mess of half-eaten organs, twisted around my oozing, exposed spinal cord. I knew at some point I would be more cancer than human.

And. I. Will. Live Through. It. All.

I wriggled around in my chemo chair, a comfy recliner, and pulled a blanket taut against my neck. I closed my eyes, feeling the chemicals as they rushed into my veins, silently praying it would only make things worse.

Static filled the room, swallowed the strangers, then swallowed me.

CHANNEL//FOURTEEN

And after a sharp quick sting of electricity, my mind was suddenly somebody else's again...

My brain was throbbing in pain, a migraine, a ticking time bomb that would never explode. It just kept ticking and ticking and ticking. Tick, tick, tick. The pain resonated from somewhere within the five sections of vertebrae between my neck and shoulders. I hopped in the shower thinking somehow it would ease the pain, after all it worked wonders on hangovers [or so I've been told]. I didn't like to rely solely on drugs, medication. If there was a chance to solve whatever ails I was experiencing in a natural manner, I preferred to do it that way. Drugs were a last resort. I laid in the bottom of the tub and let the water pour down on me from the shower head, soaking into and pruning my skin. I was an old man then, so I don't know what that makes me now.

To my surprise, the pain did not ease, in fact it had gotten worse. Much worse. The pain felt as if it had kicked and ripped apart my brain. *I thought I felt the prying fingers of a fucking ape!* The bastard was spreading apart the deep folds of my brain looking for mites, lice, or any other vermin that may have been living down inside. Pain radiated from the bones in my neck like a thousand volts of electricity and the muscles running throughout my body had stiffened and made it almost impossible to move. I managed to take hold of my head with both hands—one on my jaw, the other on my crown—and I twisted my skull in a violent rage. I meant to kill that fucking ape, but instead I felt a sharp pain, and then nothing at all. I heard the terrible sound of vertebrae slipping, shifting, and snapping. Afterwards, my world went dark.

Blindness wasn't the only thing that furious snap brought me that day, it also paralyzed my entire body. Every nerve inside me had been severed, as if I'd blown the one goddamn fuse responsible for my every movement. From that unfortunate moment on, I've been nothing but a lump, an immovable wad of lard wrapped around a tiny skeleton.

A Spanish woman named Penelope came to my aid every day after that, and she was at my side almost every hour. The government paid her to do so. *The government, ha!* She was sent by the goddamn government to spy on me, that was more like it, or at least it was my suspicion. Had a girlfriend go missing in 1978 [a long story that doesn't belong here] and they've been following me ever since. *That goddamn helper woman would steal from me!* I'd hear her quietly going through my things and the jingle-jangle of her oversized purse as she scrambled for the door. *That whore!* She fed me too much. I was a fat bloated pig because of her. Every bit of 500 pounds. *She was trying to kill me!*

In the twenty years of being this lump of flesh and bone, I'd nearly forgotten the beauty of the world. Colors faded from memory. I couldn't see color even in my own imagination, only grey. Memories were draped in the same lonely shade. When I thought of Penelope, I always imagined her to look like a grey witch, casting spells on me with her grey wand and flying around on her grey broomstick. Being blind was damn near maddening, except for fact that I became a better hearer as a result. I know they say it's just an old wives' tale, but there really is some truth to it. Maybe it's not that I'm a better hearer, per say, it's just that without my sense of sight distracting me, I notice more with my sense of hearing. Whatever the reason, I was definitely hearing things I had never heard before my blindness came.

  When the house was empty, I could hear for miles. Penelope would only leave me here alone when she thought I was asleep, so I pretended to sleep often. When she did, I could hear children playing at a playground a block away. I could hear neighbors walking their dogs [their ringing collars] outside along the streets. Those moments when I was alone were the only times I ever truly felt alive, that some small part of me was still eager to live, desiring the fruits of the world outside the prison I'd made of my own walls. However on one particular day, after Penelope left the house, I heard absolutely nothing but the humming static of the rain colliding with the earth. There was a storm brewing, and I'm not talking just a little rain either, a true storm, a dangerous storm, the type that ripped trees from roots, houses from foundations, corpses from graves [violent storms often caused cadavers buried in shallow graves to resurface, going on one final ride down the flood waters of the countryside and emptying over into some ditch or river somewhere, never to be seen again. Or at least I would have hoped for as much].

Thunder cracked overhead and shook my home. Pictures on the wall vibrated and the same vibrations traveled up my spine and reignited a flame I thought was long since gone. Chills prickled along my arms and neck as I began to feel again. Pain shot in long stems from my neck to my toes and the feeling excited me to no end. *I was able to feel again!* I wouldn't have been able to contain myself had it not been for the fact that I was still immobile, a complete vegetable. Thunder cracked again, but this time the vibrations were so powerful it caused my muscles to fully contract. *I moved.* For the first time in twenty years, I moved [however only slightly]. My neck shifted and it caused my head to fall forward a bit. It wasn't much, but it felt fantastic, completely surreal.

Hope flooded my consciousness as I waited for the next crack of the whip. The next booming thunder was even stronger than the two that had come before it. My neck muscles pulled and slung my head around like a slow-moving moon revolving around its planet, until my face was planted in the fatty pillows of my chest.

With all the excitement of moving, I hardly noticed my breathing became limited. Instead of air, I was sucking in tufts of skin. A fourth cracking thunder brought back my eyesight [lightning illuminated the room and suddenly I could see colors again, but only for a second] and sent another jolt of pain down my spine, hurling my giant body to the floor. My neck bent, this time snapping, as my head became trapped beneath the mass of blubber that was my body.

The next few hours were bliss [before Penelope would find me, that is]. The suffocation and the broken neck should have killed me, but instead I lay there on the floor, happy. The rain hummed all around me, as I finally remembered the beauty of the world.

 Penelope soon found me and I was able to breathe again, but my sight was gone [the hours without air caused some permanent damage, most noticeably my skin, now visibly displaying bright purple and blue veins, broken capillaries, prominently and disgustingly, like fleshy spiderwebs, among other minor things]. The earth continued to spin, the stars and planets still had their suns and their moons—the universe as a whole remained unchanged—however, from that moment on, I was forever different. I'd never have anyone to love or even be anyone who deserved love, but I'd always have that moment. I was happy, and although I wasn't able to physically show my feelings or my excitement, for the time being I was able to remember them, and that was good enough for me.

 The next day Penelope propped me up close to the window, and I sat there, my blind eyes pointed up at the sky, hoping to conjure up a darkness overhead. I'd sit there for days on end, eagerly awaiting the next thunderstorm.

Color bars filled my eyes and suddenly worlds were shifting again…

CHANNEL//FIVE

I drowned my ears in static, sitting beneath the giant moon on a night too cold to belong to August. My headphones served as both earmuffs and a way out, a way out of myself, even if only for minutes at a time. Noise poured out of the foamy speakers and burrowed deep into the folds of my brain, electrocuting, burning memories from the inside out. I could not think [this was a good thing]. When I say noise, I mean just that—noise—no music. I listened to sounds of light bulbs breaking, ants marching, and animals chewing. Music could not bring silence to my thoughts. No matter how mellow, it could not bring calm. Only noise. Only noise got me there.

    I felt a vibration in my pocket. It was my cell phone. The person on the other end of the line was trying to kill this moment for me, trying to bring me out of my cold night terror blues. I pretended it was supposed to happen, that it was all a part of the experience, the experience of suffocating my brain, killing myself under the bitter night's hot open mouth of spilling moonlight, overdosing on a field of vibrations with the entire universe as witness. But it wasn't working. I only felt nauseous.

I checked my phone. My friend Kayla sent me a text message. It read, "HEY BECCA, WHERE R U?"

Electric drones straddled my eardrum as I read this and I thought to myself how anyone could possibly ever answer that question accurately. *I am here*, that's where I am. That's all I know. *How could anyone know any more than that?*

"I am lost and I don't understand my existence, or even how I exist, and the moon is hanging directly above my head," I responded.

I looked up at the sky. It looked like the cold glass wall of an illuminated television screen. The stars looked like white noise to me. All in an instant I found that my eyes were suddenly drowning in static as well as my ears. There was no relief, there was no quick sharp pain or pinch to sever the nerve, only this endless drowning. Static filled my head, swelled it, but not enough. It wouldn't break. I needed more than this to escape. I was still there, inside my body. I'd done everything short of getting down on my knees and begging to be taken away, for my breath to be stolen by the vacuum, to be completely swallowed up by the ever-expanding static of the night sky. I was playing with fire and purposefully inhaling smoke.

My phone vibrated again. Kayla said, "FUNNY YOU MENTION THE MOON, IT'S ALL OVER THE NEWS TONIGHT."

I tried my best to ignore her, to continue with my lunar suicide, but I found the message too strange not to reply. I drummed my fingers across my leg and thought about tossing my phone out into the dark ocean of tall grass that surrounded me, but only for a second. I refrained.

"What do you mean?" I typed.

I buried my hands in my pockets, frustrated at the entire universe, myself included. There was a pressure in my skull, a pressure that could only be cured by death. Everyone I knew had let me down, even my own body had failed me. I chose to pass on, to continue living life in my next form, a form without this…*pressure*, but I couldn't do it alone. Believe me, I've tried, but time and time again I've failed. I was too strong for death, it seemed. Time would pass, every single night, failure after failure, and I would look up at the moon and the man inside would grin his unusual grin and stare down at me with crow's feet clipped to his eyelids. I'd be sitting in a pool of my own blood, vomit, shit, and the moon would just smile, mocking my pathetic, useless, never-ending existence.

I looked up at the moon with more anger than hope. The noise swelled inside my skull, but it was not enough. Nothing was ever enough. The cold stuck to the skin of my face like a thousand tiny needles. I was feeling numb, but again, not enough. The giant moon was full and bright and looming. I continued to taunt it, to stare back at it with eyes that were filled not with fear, but anger. I could not see the man inside the moon that night and it had me wondering if I ever would again.

That goddamn moon owed me this. After all, it was the primary cause of my cranial pressure. It gave me nothing but pain in my twenty-eight years, and all I'd done in that time was try to ignore it, or at times when I was feeling extra ambitious, run away from it, but not that night. That night I was asking to finally be put out of my misery.

And it failed me, of course. Like everything else in this goddamn universe had failed me. Tears were forming at the corners of my eyes. I couldn't handle any more pressure. If only I could have fallen to my knees, pressed a loaded gun to the end of my nostrils, and pulled the trigger. If only I could have sent a cold bullet of relief straight through the pain, a one-way ticket out of myself forever...but I couldn't and wouldn't. *So many flaws.*

My phone vibrated again. I wiped the tears from my eyes and checked the screen. It read, "NEIL ARMSTRONG IS DEAD."

I decided not to respond this time. I put the phone in my pocket and laid down in the grass, continuing to gaze up at the moon. Suddenly I wasn't angry anymore. I'd managed to calm myself down, *or rather Kayla had*. If it took forty-three years for the moon to finally get to Neil, then I guess I had around fifteen more of my own left at least. It wasn't the answer I was looking for, but it was an answer nonetheless. It may not have been the immediate reprieve of the pressure I needed, but it was a time frame, maybe more like a prison sentence, so I couldn't be angry over it. There was an end in sight. A darkness at the end of the tunnel.

Sometimes I'd get so caught up in my own troubles that I'd forget about the troubles of others, that there were other people in the world suffering too, not just me. I needed to learn to be more patient, more considerate. The moon had a big job. I'm sure it killed dozens on any given night—and though I couldn't guarantee it, I'd be willing to bet they'd all been suffering much longer than I had. I must have been close though, to see the man inside as he stared down at me from above. Seemed too odd to be a coincidence. I must have been within reach in those moments, but he was not there that night, the night I called him out, and at the time it was all that mattered.

I took off my headphones.

I could wait.

I pulled out my phone and wrote back to Kayla. "I wonder if Neil got the chance to look Apollo in the eye tonight?"

After a few seconds passed, Kayla responded.

"YOU SHOULD COME OVER."

All at once, a great deal of pressure faded. I stood up and walked away from the moon.

Static. Stati—

[32] IF YOU DON'T SLEEP, YOU DON'T DREAM.

In many ways, Adam's story destroys me. No matter how many times I see it, the way it loops continuously inside my mind, I feel myself aching for him in a way I don't for the others. Turning the dial to channel thirty-two, I was able to catch part of his story I had never seen before, a nightmare taking place much later in his life, as an old man. Seeing him like this, scarred, disassembled, reassembled, broken and suffering, actually brought physical pain to witness. At least xxxxxx took away his memories. He would have had to, as no man could withstand the physical torture he was forced to endure while also suffering from such crippling mental anguish. That surely would have reached a depth of madness never before seen in man. As he said before, a man is dangerous without his family, though then he surely had no idea what was to become of him. Oh, Adam, here's to hoping you never remember all you've lost...

I

Gunshots.
Gunshots!
I hear men screaming!
I can hear them!
Three at least!
They're dying!
Screaming for God!
Gordon?
I'm scared.
Scared.
Scared.
What do they want from us?
What is it they want?
What do they want from us, Gordon?

Where are you?
Do they have you?
Are you there, Gordon?
Are you there?
Gordon, please God, Gordon?
Gordon is gone.
Gordon is gone.
This room is empty.
Gordon is gone.
I need to leave.
I'm leaving.
I need to find Gordon.
My eye!
Where did I leave my eye?
False, it is. Pure white.
A gift from Gordon.
Now where...
The cupboards?
The stove?
The mug!
Yes, the mug is where I left my eye! Haha!
Cold, it is... icy water.
Goddamned winter.
Freezing my socket.
Goddamn this room.
Goddamn this building.
I'd kill just for the body heat.

It's so goddamn cold.
The front door is frozen shut.
I beat the piss out of it.
I beat the living hell out of it.
Ice is breaking.
Falling to my boots.
The letter.
I see the letter.
The letter from Gordon.
I see the letter.
I never want to read.
Gordon always leaves me.
Gordon always leaves me *here*.
I never want to read.
Never.
Forever in my pocket.
Never will I read.
I break open the door.
There is a box outside.
Lazarus.
My name.
Written on the box.
It's from Gordon.
He's left me again.
Gordon is gone.
In the box?
Happiness.

Enough to last while Gordon is gone.
I hope.

> *Dear God! Help us!*

There is a man lying down in the hall, screaming.
He is bleeding.
Dying.
But is he asking for me or asking for God?
I should leave.

> ...

Gordon?
I must find Gordon.
I turn and look at the man, bleeding, terrified, cold, but I must find Gordon.
I cannot stop.

> *Hey, you! We need help! Call an ambulance!*

> ...

Please, old man, help us.

I look back.
The man is pointing a gun at me.
I walk toward him.
He is young.
Much younger than me.
Maybe thirty... forty years-old.
He is not alone.
In Gordon's room there are two others.
Neither are moving.
Blood pours from their lifeless bodies.
Did you do this Gordon? Did you take these lives?
There is a gold badge hanging from the dying man's belt.
He grabs at his chest.

*Look, I don't want to hurt you...
it's just we need help and you were
walking away.*

Are... you... a police... officer?

My voice.
Raspy and weak.
Always out of breath, I am.

> *Detective.*
> *John Gray.*
> *We came to bust this guy... Gordon.*
> *Somehow he knew we were coming.*

He clutched his hand over his heart, as if he could touch
his pain and remove it
violently tearing it away.
Shot three times.
One in each leg and another in the right side of his chest.
Walking closer to Detective Gray,
I notice him wince.
He can't stand the horror of my malformed face.
A hideous beast, I am!
Unworthy to breathe, I am!
Gordon, He never winced.
Gordon, my only friend.
I touch the cavernous trenches of my scarred face.

> I know... a wretched beast... I am.
> But I... I wouldn't be... alive...
> if not for... Gordon. He saved... me.

The detective traces the scars with his perfect-working eyes, trying to make sense of their placement.
What happened to him, he wonders.
Forever wonders.
His eyes clamp shut.
His chest... the pain is too much.
He clenches his fists.

Agghh... God! Can you find a phone?
I think Dodd had one, he's the one on the left, check his pockets...

I walk over to Dodd.
Stone-cold Dodd.
Half his head blown across the room.
Parts of him stuck to the walls and ceiling.
I dig my hand into the pockets of dead Dodd's jacket.
I find a toothpick, a wallet, a bag of pistachios, and a cell phone.
Before taking the phone back to Detective Gray, I walk over to the closet and grab Gordon's toolbox.

The toolbox has everything needed to
perform an emergency surgery of any kind:
scalpels, hammers (of all sizes), a chisel,
clamps, a staple gun...
Anything a doctor would ever need.

>Gordon... Gordon... is a good... man.
>He... helps me.

Dear God, what has he done to you?

I walk back over to Detective Gray, his skin
growing pale,
I hand him the phone.
I open the toolbox and shuffle through its
contents.
The detective dials for help, eyeballing my
every move.
The detective is having trouble speaking.
He pauses.

Thanks...

*This is Detective
John Gray. We need an ambulance...
Three men down. Possibly two dead.*

200 Archer Avenue
The old Peterson building.
We're on the seventeenth floor.

I walk into Gordon's kitchen and grab a glass of warm water and stir in a cup of salt.
I quickly walk back into the hallway.
Detective Gray, no longer on the phone, is now applying pressure to the wound in his chest, taking in quick, deep breaths.
He coughs and blood fills his mouth,
his tongue drowning, sloshing within the gore, his teeth pale pink.
He spits on the carpet.
The detective looks up at me.

Did you get... help?

Yeah... an ambulance will be here in five to ten minutes.

I fumble frantically through the toolbox, looking for tweezers.
The detective coughs again, spitting more blood on the carpet.

What are you doing?

You need... help.

I'm getting—
I'm getting help.

You need help... now... or you will... die.

Frustrated with searching, I dump the contents of the toolbox onto the floor of the hallway.

Here... we go.

I hold up a large pair of surgical steel tweezers.
I dig the tips into his chest wound.
About two and a half inches deep, I can feel the metal of the tweezers scraping against the metal of the bullet.
Metal on metal.
I can feel it, hear it—blood seeps and now I even taste it.

I let up on my grasp, allowing the tweezers to pull apart the wound just enough for me to slide the tips down each side of the bullet.
Blood pools and I see nothing but mirrored red, bright and blinding.
I feel around with the end of the tweezers, get a grip on the bullet, and pull it straight out of the wound.
Detective Gray, who held his breath for the entirety, finally exhales at the sight of the flattened shrapnel exiting his body.
Gore gushes from the wound with each heartbeat, spattering across my grey trench coat.
I don't mind.
Never do I mind.
I pour the warm salt water into the wound.
Detective Gray howls.

Jesus.
FUCK!

The salt... it will clean it.
Slow the... bleeding.

I pull out a needle and thread from Gordon's toolbox and begin to sew the detective's chest wound shut.
It is silent now.
The detective tries not to look down at my crooked fingers working away.
Instead, he speaks.
I look up at him, puzzled.
My fingers slow.
My eye wide.
Gordon.

Why were you going to leave?
Why weren't you going to help us?

Detective Gray looks at me.
He wants me to speak.
The detective looks into my eye, my left eye, my one good eye.
He nods then loses consciousness.

Gordon, where have you gone?
Gordon.
He is all I have.

A door swings open violently down the
hallway behind us.
The doorknob buries itself into the
deteriorating sheet rock,
serving as an anchor, allowing the paramedics
and police officers to scuttle through the
doorway like a raging stampede.
Immediately I am thrown belly down onto the
floor by an enraged police officer.
He thinks I'm Gordon.
Two of his kind are dead.
I understand his frustration.
I don't resist.
The paramedics surround Detective Gray.
The police officers surround the cadavers.

You'll burn in Hell for this!

You'll burn in Hell for this.
It's the last thing I will hear tonight.
The officer plows an elbow into my face.
The impact causes two of my rotted teeth to
tear through the soft tissue of my cheek.
My eye, my left eye, my one good eye
sees only white.

II

I am awake in a cell.
Jail or prison? I do not know.
The stone walls are wet with night air.
A massive iron door is placed between the world and me.
A massive iron door protects the entire human race from me.
Me! Lazarus!
Ha! An old fucking man, I am!
This impenetrable cell wasted on such old bones!
Of all the hatred, terrors, horrors in the world,
This cell is wasted on *me!*
Time has no presence in this place.
The sun, the moon may as well not even exist.
I count the days as they pass by the number of meals I am served.
So far seventeen... nearly six days.
I haven't had any medication.
My stomach churns.
I never eat the meals they bring me.
Only the bread.

A migraine pulses through the tiny nerves in my brain with such violence I fear my skull will split in two.
The only relief comes from vomiting water and bile when the pain becomes impossible.
Gordon warned me about not taking my medicine.
But I didn't *forget!*
I just don't have it.
I may never have it again.
I may never see Him again.
Get used to it, I should.
So, I lay here in my cell.
I shouldn't expect anything, I know, but I find myself waiting.
For Him.

The heavy metal slot on my iron door unlocks and slides, revealing the tired old eyes of the night guard.

You have a visitor.

Who?

Gordon.

Gordon.
Gordon.

Just get on your feet, old man.

I obey his request and the guard slides the lock and opens the heavy door.
He takes me from my cell down a long and dark hallway.
There are a total of eight other iron doors, just like mine down this hallway.
In the distance, a guard calls for lights out.
Then it hits me.
Lights out...
It's too late for visitors.
Gordon would never see me here... a wanted man!
He would have to be insane to show His face here.
Gordon is no loon.
Panic sends its death shock through to the tips of my every nerve.
I scream, as loud as an old man can, and am quickly silenced.

The officer hurls me face-first into the stone brick wall and presses cold blue steel to my temple.

> *Look, fuckface, if it were up to me I'd splatter your goddamn brains out right here all over this wall. But it ain't up to me...*

He pulls his gun away and shoves me down the hall.

> *Now shut the fuck up and walk.*

The officer leads me into an empty interrogation room:
a two-way mirror, a swinging light fixture, just like on television.
I take a seat at the table in the middle of the room.
Another door opens.
It's Detective Gray.
He is in a wheelchair with a bandage across his chest and a cast on each leg.

Hey, buddy... remember me?

I remember.

They tell me your name is Lazarus.

They are... correct.

The detective laughs at my awkwardness.

Well, first I want to say thank you...
you saved my life.
The doc said if you hadn't been there that night
then I would have been buried on Tuesday
along with my partners.

I nod, staring blankly, concentrating more on the painful swelling of my brain than to the detective's words.
I move my eye to meet his.
The detective sighs.

And second... I want to apologize.

*They didn't tell me that you were
arrested until earlier today
when I was released from the hospital.
I've already spoken to the warden
and he is filing the necessary paperwork to
get you released as soon as possible.*

I can go... home?

*Uh... not quite.
The experts here feel you aren't capable
of living on your own.
There are also a few doctors who are
very interested in your...
you know, 'condition'.*

My condition?

*They want to know what Gordon has done to you,
Lazarus.
They can help you.*

Detective Gray's face begins to melt.
His skin liquefies and slides off his skull,

streaming down his neck and soaking into the collar of his shirt.
My vision blurs.
I close my eye tight and reboot.
His face is restored.

>I need my medication.

>*Medication?*

>'Happiness', Gordon has me take it...
every day.

>*Happiness?*

>It keeps visions away... I have demons.

>*Where would one find this medicine?*

>In my room... my home... there is a box...
Lazarus, it will say. LAZARUS.
In heavy black ink.
Written by the pen of my father,
my only friend...

My eye wells and a tear streams down my cheek.
The detective raises a suspicious brow.
Gordon.
Gordon is gone.

Gordon is your father?

Yes.

How old are you, Lazarus?

Fifty.

Fifty? Wow, really?
Don't take offense, but I had you pegged at about eighty or ninety.
Fifty. You know, I'll be forty-five next month. Are you saying that you're only five years older than me?

Questions, questions.
Always questions.

Fifty.

> *Fifty... okay.*
> *Well, the reason I ask*
> *is because this guy Gordon...*
> *he's fifty-nine years old.*

My eye meets his and quickly pulls away to the left.

> *So that would have made Gordon nine years old*
> *when you were born, does that sound about right?*

I don't answer his questions.
Always with questions!
His suspicious, perfect-working eyes!
His motor-mouth!
I want him silenced!
No answer, you fool!
Swine!

> *I call bullshit.*
> *You're much older than you're leading on and*
> *there's no way in hell that Gordon is your father.*
> *You're hiding something, Lazarus...*

Look, I understand I owe you.
But I still have a job to do, Lazarus.
You got that?

Stupid, pig-fucking mule!

I'm going to get you your medicine, but if anyone asks,
you didn't get it from me.
I'll do this one thing, but that's it.
I'm going to find Gordon and have his ass fried
even if it's the last goddamn thing I—

I leap across the table and dig my nails into
the never silent throat of Detective Gray.
For three full seconds I feel a rush of
adrenaline flowing through my veins and
emptying out through my fingertips.
Two officers burst into the room and pull me
off the handicapped detective.
Skin beneath my nails.
Bloody fingers.
I had his life in my hands!
Bastard wants to kill my father!
My only friend!
Gordon...

The officers force me to walk down another
hallway, different than the one I came
through just minutes before.
A feeling of terror calms my rage.

> Where are you... taking me?

> *You're going to solitary.*
> *You've got to be the*
> *dumbest motherfucker alive, old man.*
> *Assaulting a police officer!*
> *Are you serious?*

The two officers push me into a dark room
and slam
the heavy door shut.
The lock snaps in place.
I hear their laughs grow faint as they walk
away.
Again I am alone.
Always alone.

Gordon?

III

The dark, she plays tricks on the eyes, she does.
Night is the earth's eyelids.
So many sights I've seen in the night!
First the frogs…
They poured down like heavy rain from the pipes above.
Giant bullfrogs with three rows of teeth.
Razor-wire teeth, they had.
Hungry for the blood of the weak.
Me! I was the weak.
I was able to squeeze the life from the first few, but as the numbers grew, I wasn't able to kill them fast enough.
It was over at first bite.
That first taste of blood was enough to drive them mad!
They ripped every tendon from its bone.
I collapsed to the wet floor, no muscle to stand.
They leapt onto my back, ripping into flesh like lions feasting.
Finding my face, they dug fangs an inch deep, pulling muscle and gore from the bloody skull that lay beneath.

One frog plucked out my right eye, not knowing it was false—choked and died.
I laughed at the sight, grateful for this one small victory, before finally submitting to the enemy.
Then I awoke, as I always would after such strange visions, laying still in the dark.

Another of these visions occurred shortly after the first, this time taking me out of my darkened cell entirely and into a colder world surrounded by mountains of snow and ice.
Standing in front of me, eyes frozen, almost glass, was Gordon.
He wasn't combed or shaven.
He was smiling. Eerily smiling.
He was calm.
He never blinked.
We both stood and stared at each other in silence for several moments.
Finally He spoke:

Sleep...my mind begs for it, but my eyes..
they always seem to wander...
endlessly... aimlessly...
I'm not certain why the world focuses on such petty matters.
We all should be preparing for the future.

> *Beasts, that as of now only exist to us in fairy tale,
> will be stampeding the earth with a hunger for blood.
> The Devil is in the waiting.
> Surely someone feels his presence.*

In the vision, I knew exactly what Gordon
was trying to tell me.
In the real world, I wasn't sure.
Gordon spoke of the Devil as if He witnessed
his decent into Hell.
Gordon spoke of God as if he were dead.
He always spoke of a revelation, a rapture...
but never in those words, and never in the
typical Christian perspective.
Instead He spoke of the Devil's reign on
Earth as if it were imminent,
within our lifetime.
How demons would dig up the earth, out of
Hell and through the yards of our neighbors
to devour their sons and rape their daughters.
Sometimes I was convinced He was an
angel—Gordon.
He knew the design of the human body as if
He Himself had helped God create us.
The miracles... the miracles this man has
performed!

As if He had the specific blueprints in his head, it was!
Complete knowledge of anatomy and physiology, He had.
Like no other doctor before Him.
And the miracles He has performed on me, Lazarus...
I was born again.
My scars all necessary.
I would not be here without Gordon.
I would not be.

Gordon not only had the blueprints, He improved them.
He enhanced my body in ways no earthly doctor could.
Through all the surgeries and medications, Gordon gave me everlasting life.
And Detective Gray hopes to kill this blessed man.
I will bury his black bones before I ever let him bring harm to Gordon.

Returning to the vision:
After Gordon spoke His last word,
He began to decompose.

His skin and bones rotted before my eyes.
His jawbone was the last to fall, landing on the pile of ash that was quickly taken by the wind.
He was gone.
Gordon... always gone.
Always leaving.
I was again left in the dark.
The dark.
Such vile, rotten things come from the dark.

I lay on stone now.
My cell is cold.
I don't feel the walls, or even sense their presence.
I feel removed...from myself, my body, and this cell.
My eye starts twitching, peeking, focusing.
Finally there is light.
Dim, she is, but still light.
A dark figure stands before me, unfocused.
The dark, she lives inside me.
Focusing, focusing... but the dark is still inside me fighting, trying to kill it.
The figure, she is a woman... crying, full of fear.
She puts a hand to her mouth.

The dark pulls its shade and I sleep.

Adam…

My mind becomes electric.

IV

I am awake and alert.
I am in a hospital room surrounded by noisy machines, the smell of coffee, 3AM.
I am nervous.
I am nervous because I am in pain.
I am in pain because all my scars have been reopened.
I have a beard and slightly longer hair than when I first fell asleep.
Something has happened to me.
A nurse walks in.
The scene curdles her blood.
She turns and walks out the door.
A doctor steps in moments later.
He is prepared to look at me.
He does not shudder.

How are you feeling?

I'm so nervous I'm trembling.

That bad, huh?
Well, you're going to need your rest,
so I'll make this brief.
You've been drifting in and out of a coma for nearly
three weeks now.
In that time we've run a few tests and found many
peculiarities with your condition.

My condition.
Again, 'my condition'.

This guy, Gordon, he has really done a
number on you.
We've found foreign materials in nine
areas of your body,
many serving no mortal purpose,
but rather seem to have
been placed for his own amusement.

…

*Are you aware your body has been wired
to be accessed and controlled via remote control?*

R-r-r-remote... c-c-c-control?

*Yes, there were mechanisms, which we've disabled,
located in your hands and feet
that were equipped to receive radio commands
and were cabled throughout your body
via a confusing and
complicated hardwire setup.
We also found peculiar
machine parts located in your heart,
your left forearm, your inner thigh on your right leg,
between your shoulder blades, and your brain.*

A living autopsy.

*Although we weren't able to pinpoint the exact
function of many of these machines,
we were able to quickly identify the purpose of and
remove, what
we've been calling, the 'spider implant'.
The body of the spider implant was located*

*in the frontal lobe of
your brain with several 'legs'
reaching across and pinching sections
responsible for retaining long-term memory.
We simply traced your scars
when making our incisions,
as to not cause any further scarring.*

W-w-w-hy w-would I
c-c-care about sc-c-carring?

The doctor laughs.
I'm confused.

How am I... alive?
How could I have
possibly...survived this?

I don't honestly know. But here you are.

You risked me dying?

*To be fair, you are in far better shape now
than you were when you arrived.
You were not well when you came into this building.*

For that, you're welcome.

The doctor gives a half-smile and sighs.

> *Okay... okay. This is a lot to take in all in one sitting.*
> *Why don't you get some rest and I'll come check on you after a bit?*

I nod.
The doc gives me the other half of the smile and exits the room.
I study the seeping faults interrupting my skin in disgust.
Such a wretch, I am!
To be beaten and burned, I deserve!

It's then that I notice the neatly wrapped box sitting on the table next to me.
I reach over and pick it up.
The tag reads: *"To Lazarus... Now we're even."*
I rip off the wrapping, and beneath, a familiar box.
LAZARUS. It reads.
LAZARUS. In heavy black ink.

Written by the pen of my father, my only friend... Gordon.
I remove a syringe from the box and push out the air bubbles.
I take out my right eye, my glass eye, and inject 40mL of
Happiness directly into my frontal lobe, through the empty socket.
My body begins to convulse and spasm!
Never once has this happened!
I am supposed to be free!
The machines that surround me begin to howl and soon doctors and nurses enter.
They poke and prod at me, this living corpse, in hopes to find an answer.
An answer to silence the machines.
An answer to what they've found beneath my scars.
An answer that must be given by *me*.

V

Gordon sets his suitcase down on the armchair.
He looks at me with fire.
We are in a seedy motel room—the air is thick with mold.

A voice in my head whispers the year, 1978, but the month escapes me.
Gordon, always smiling, bends down and snaps open the suitcase.
He steps back.
The two halves of the heavy suitcase separate about an inch, then fall shut again.
Something is living inside it, *someone*.
He takes perch behind the armchair so He can see both me and the case, His smile sometimes slipping into marvelous, excited yelps.
The suitcase opens again slightly and a woman's frail,
delicate hand slides through.
My eye widens with shock, shifting between Gordon and the hand and back again.
I don't know what to do, I am frozen with fright!
Gordon, hardly able to contain Himself, speeds the process by lifting the suitcase top away for her.
The woman lifts her head slowly and looks around the room, somehow overlooking us both.

She pushes her upper body up and out of the case; her long dark hair falls onto her shoulders.
She is silent.
Her head bobs and jerks as the anesthesia Gordon gave her slowly begins to wear off. She is wearing nothing but a short white silk nightgown and a pair of pale pink panties.
Her legs are numb.
She carelessly throws herself to the floor, suitcase tumbling after.
She throws her head up and wrenches herself forward with her hands, collapsing after only one strenuous pull.
Her body lays limp.
Finally she gains enough strength to pull up to her knees, but is still paralyzed at the legs.
Gordon steps out from behind the armchair, slowly walking towards her.
He looks up at me and places a finger to His grin, signaling for me to keep quiet, as He reveals an ice pick menacingly clutched in His hand.
The woman weeps.
Her innocent wail plucks at my heartstrings, falling silent now by Gordon's insensitive hand.

He pushes the pick into her, hard and quick.
It digs deep into the back of her skull, but somehow does not kill her.
Gordon is precise in His ways.
If He wants her alive, she will remain alive.
If He wants silence, then silent she'll be.
If He doesn't want her to remember, you better believe she won't remember a thing.
Gordon grabs a hold of the woman's long dark hair in His fist and pulls her to her feet.
He turns His attention to me.
Smiling again.
Always smiling.

Ready?
Are you ready, Laz?

Ready for what... Gordon?

Gordon howls and tosses the woman onto the bed.
The woman looks at us in horror.
Gordon crawls on top of her and drags His slimy tongue across her cheek.
He grabs a handful of her hair and breathes the stench of her sweat into His lungs.

Gordon looks into her eyes, revealing His intentions without saying a word.
I hesitate.
Gordon whips His head around and stares at me with wicked eyes and immediately I cower and give in, hoping if I comply He'll return His attention to the girl.
A coward, I am.
I loosen the button on my pants and they fall to my ankles.
Gordon takes hold of the woman's silk nightgown in both hands and rips the material from her body exposing her naked breasts and torso.
The woman is screaming inside.
I can see the fear in her eyes.
Gordon rips the panties from her trembling hips and spreads her legs wide open.

And now to plant the seed, Laz.

Completely powerless, I am.
I obey His command.
Gordon, still holding her legs, watches as I penetrate her.
I'm raping her.

She's raping me.
Two people having sex against our will.
The blood trickling from the hole in her head soaks the sheets as I pump my hips.
She's paralyzed.
Tears run down her temples from the corners of her eyes.

Ahhhh...

When I finish, I run to the bathroom and vomit into the commode.

I'd like to think this was only a dream, but the doctors here tell me these dreams and visions are actually memories releasing into my conscience as my frontal lobe heals.
And believe them, I do.
They are too real.
Too terrifying.
I am ashamed of the memories that have returned over the last week.
More than ashamed, completely disgusted.
The hospital transferred me here to the sleep clinic after I had complained of severe

nightmares, one of which lasted for seventeen hours.
Unable to awaken, I was!
Memories tear out from the depths of my brain and alter my reality and self-perception.
Torture, it is!
Pure Hell!
Put an end to it, I will!
I will never sleep again!

It takes over two hours for a doctor to see me.
The clinic is much different than the hospital in that way.
At the hospital I was able to get a nurse or doctor at any given notice.
Here, they couldn't care less.
If I were to die here in this room, I likely wouldn't be found until hours later when room service arrives.
I'm exaggerating, of course, but at times it felt like a ghost town.
The doctor finally walks in, keeping his arms crossed so that he can easily glance at the face of his watch without making it too obvious to me.
Wasting his time, I am.

I understand you wish to speak with me?

Yes...
I want to be... put on medication.

Oh, really? What sort of medication?

Something to keep me awake...

Awake?

You did good, Laz, my boy!
You made Daddy proud!

Lazarus, this is a sleep clinic!

I know this... but I'm afraid... of my dreams.

The doctor laughs.

*Our purpose in studying your dreams is
to find out more about this... Gordon.
There is absolutely no way we can do that with you
awake.
If you don't sleep, you don't dream.*

> Yes… exactly. I am afraid.

> *Look, I'm sorry.*
> *There's nothing I can do about it.*

My eye sees only red.

> *I have other patients to attend to.*
> *Is there anything else you need?*

I shake my head.

> *Try and have a nice night, Lazarus.*
> *I'll be speaking with you when you wake up*
> *tomorrow morning.*

The doctor exits the room.
The thought occurs to me that perhaps they are lying.
Perhaps the dreams are only dreams and they are just trying to get me to turn against Gordon.
Pulled me away, they did!
He may have come back for me!

Inject me with drugs and speak into my ears as I sleep, they do!
Turning the cogs while I dream!
Making me feel in control when I have no control...
I will show them!
Find Gordon on my own, I will!

Later that night a nurse comes to prep me for the sleep exam.
Just before she injects me with the prescribed sleeping meds, I leap to my feet and jam the syringe into her neck.
The nurse falls limply to the floor.
I drag her body into the bathroom.
I walk down the many empty hallways, dodging two night watchmen standing by the door.
They are talking, laughing, watching TV.
They don't even notice as I exit the building.
This is my escape.
Much easier than I'd anticipated.
But again, this is no prison, just an ordinary understaffed clinic.

I set out on the dark streets of the city.
Gordon is out here somewhere.
Find him, I will.

I reach into my pocket and pull out the letter Gordon left for me on the night of the gunshots.
The night I saved the life of that unappreciative Detective Gray.
My hands tremble in anger as I unfold the letter.

Only seven words appear on the page, scrawled by hand in black marker:

I will wait for you in Hell.

[23] The Jelly Pumps

Sometimes this dial goes back and forth, past and present flickers to the point that I actually become lost inside each timeline, unaware of what came first or who lived before who or if any of us are still living today. Though their lives play out as immaculate visions inside my brain, I still identify each of us as separate people. Do they exist outside of me? Have they ever existed at all? I do not know. I'm not even sure how many of us are still living and how many have since passed on, though it seems we all lead unusual lives that never seem to end, all of us sharing this one unique gift...this curse.

The visions loop continuously, which I assume means at some point their lives have all ended, if not, then what is the purpose of replaying these scenes over and over again? If their lives indeed have ended, the visions of their deaths have yet to play out inside my head. In all five of these lives, I have yet to witness a clear-cut end. Perhaps this is why I feel so compelled to turn the dial...

She said, "Let's go to the ocean," and twenty minutes later we were headed east. We were driving so fast, the stars flew by our ears, looking more like lines on the road than heavens for men. The wind blew through our hair and we waved our arms outside the windows, pretending we were giant soaring birds. We didn't fly, but I felt we came close. I studied her face as she drove, as best I could in the darkness, hardly believing I was falling madly in love with a *girl*. I wondered what my parents would think if they knew their daughter was bi-sexual, or perhaps even a full-blown lesbian [hell, I wasn't even sure what to call myself, or how I *felt* about it]. Surely they'd be surprised, just as I was surprised to discover so myself. It wasn't *all* girls that made me feel this way, though, or any other girl for that matter. Only her. She was the only person I ever truly wanted to know.

A song played on the stereo called "Your Funeral, My Trial" and I stared at the sky, my face basking in the pale moonlight, as the man on the radio sang about his guilt, his shame, and I looked at the moon as he sang about her, how her beauty was worthless, and I felt the same. We listened to the song on repeat until we caught up to the end of the world: the ocean, the salty sea. I hadn't seen it in so long. So many years wasted on other things— other loves, other feelings, other beauties—but nothing compared to this, this moment here with her at the edge of the earth. Nothing ever came close.

Haley wrecked her car as she pulled in to park. She failed to brake as she turned into the lot, crushing the front end against the only streetlamp in sight for miles, which now angled outward a good forty-five degrees. The light hanging over us flittered and strobed before finally burning out completely. Our only light now came from the full moon above, in all its superficial glory. We opened our doors and stepped out onto the pavement. Smoke rolled out from under the hood and the engine popped and cracked like rocks in a campfire.

It felt great to be so far away from home.

I grabbed Haley's hand and we climbed the small hill that stood between us and the shore. The hill was thick with grass and soaking up the early morning dew. We took turns picking each other up as we slipped our way to the top, the sounds of the ocean sloshed into my ears, teasing us with its call. The grass was tallest at the top, as if someone out there in the night was trying to hide the ocean from us.

But we found it.

And it was ours...for one glorious hour.

We took off our shoes and stepped onto the sand. I sunk into the damp earth, the sand oozing between my toes, before burying them completely. Not that I could see them anyway, the entire planet had been dipped in darkness. The moon allowed me to see the outline of Haley's body, but not much else. I remember her appearing more beautiful to me in that moment then she ever had before. This one memory, this single image of her bathing in the moonlight, looking over at me, pulling her hair back behind her ears and smiling, still haunts me to this day.

I don't have her anymore, but that part comes later.

The black ocean crashed upon the shore, sounding like a television gone to static. I closed my eyes and became hypnotized by the sound. I lifted my arms to the sky and let the fierce cold wind crack its whips down upon me. I was a slave to the elements in that moment. I knew better than to believe in peace, but in that moment I was feeling something that felt close enough to it to call it that. The night felt electric. My feet felt rooted inside a mechanical earth. I was part of the machine, part of its strange nature, a human somehow evolving and de-evolving all at once. I felt closeness, I heard the heartbeat of god in the soil. Haley felt it too, I could see it in her eyes, but we said nothing to each other about it. She grabbed my hand and we walked along the edge of the earth with only the sounds of the ocean to guide us.

Haley was the first to see them. Out about a hundred feet from the shore there were strange yellow lights, hundreds of them. They seemed to be moving closer to us, and growing in numbers. We sat down on the sand, wrapped our arms around each other, and waited for them to reach the shore.

"I think it's a submarine," she said, breaking minutes of silence.

"No way. The lights are too sporadic to be any kind of craft," I said, squeezing her sides in my arms. "Whatever they are, they're alive."

She seemed scared after that. I didn't notice right away, but once the lights finally reached the shore it became obvious. She leapt to her feet and sprinted back for her shoes. I laughed and grabbed her by the ankle and she fell down against the sand.

"Let me go!" she screamed, kicking her feet at my hands. I wrapped my arms around her and told her it was okay.

"They're jellyfish," I said, as the living lights washed up on the shore.

She calmed and we sat there as the ocean spewed these lovely creatures out onto the sand all around us. Soon we were surrounded by hundreds of them, their little yellow bodies flashing as if the sands were on fire, all of them out of time of one another. It was an incredible sight, almost as beautiful as the vision of Haley under the moonlight, but nowhere near as painful.

I looked over at her, her face fully visible now from the jellyfish glow of the sands. I loved her. It was in that moment that I first really knew for sure. I should have told her. I would have, if I knew then that the hour was to be the last I'd ever share with her.

The sun was rising over the water. I could smell the ocean absorbing the sunlight. The two of us had a thousand reasons to go back home that very minute, but we didn't leave. Instead, we sat and watched the sun as it came up out of the ocean. As daylight began to crack through the once solid night sky, Haley dug deep into her purse and pulled out a small wooden box. It was worn at the edges, suggesting the box was old, perhaps even older than Haley. There were dark grooves that ran along the top, outlining the image of a serpent.

"What's this?" I asked.

"Happiness," she replied. It was the last word she ever said, to me, to anyone.

She threw her purse in the direction of our shoes, looked at me and smiled. The pink rays of sunlight slid over her face as if she were peeking out at me from behind a set of window blinds. She closed her eyes and we kissed. Her taste was salty, like the sea. I thought then that maybe it was just the mist rolling off the ocean that made her taste this way, but now looking back, I can't help but wonder if I tasted death on her tongue that night. How badly I wished I had taken her there on the shore and tasted every part of her until there was enough death in me to have gone with her. *But wishes never brought death, I'd come to realize.*

She opened the box. Five syringes were inside, complete with needles. I was shocked. I didn't know she was a user. In fact, it was at that moment that I realized I didn't really know much about her at all. I was in love with a complete stranger. I wanted to ask her what the needles were for, hoping for an answer different than what I was assuming, but before I could, she was up on her feet and walking toward one of the beached electric jellyfish. All in a single motion, she took a syringe and pierced the skin of one of the creatures. She pulled back on the plunger and withdrew as much glowing yellow jellyfish blood the tube could hold, then pulled out.

She handed it to me. I took it. I should have done anything else, but I took it. I held it as she filled another for herself. When she was finished, she flicked the syringe, emptying any pockets of oxygen hidden inside. I did the same. I should have done anything else, but I did the same. We kissed one final time, the heat from the rising sun warming our necks, before she stepped back, out of our kiss, and dove headfirst into darkness. She took it all. Every bit. Every drop of glowing electric jelly was emptied into her veins. She collapsed and fell to the sand before even removing the needle from her arm.

I should have picked her up.

I should have removed the needle.

I should have done anything else, but I did nothing.

She went into a coma the moment the jelly got to her heart. She continued to breathe for maybe ten minutes after that, but it was difficult, complicated breathing. Blood leaked from her mouth, her nose, the corners of her eyes. I did nothing but sit there, staring at the needle full of jelly in my hand, and contemplate whether or not I should lay there and die with her.

    I was a coward.

    Always a coward.

    I sat next to her until the moment her heart stopped beating. Soon after, the waves came crashing to the shore, and when they returned, they dragged her body into the dark water. A burial at sea.

    There was nowhere to go but home, so I went, taking only my memories of her in our short time together. I never stopped thinking of her. Some forty odd years later, and I could still smell her perfume as I stood there on the edge of the land, staring off into the sea. The smell of salt reminded me of her kiss, her taste. To taste Haley was to taste death itself.

    When I finally returned to the shore, so many years later [Haley, it took *decades* to get the courage], I walked the places we walked. I saw they fixed the streetlamp she hit with her car and it brought a smile to my face. I climbed the hill and walked through the wall of grass hiding the beach. As soon as my toes touched the sand, I fell to my knees. Somehow I was tasting her, there on the shore, with all those years between us. I hadn't expected that. The saltiness on my tongue felt sharp, piercing, painful. Guilt crept up my throat and I nearly vomited there on the sand.

I should have returned to my car and drove home, but I didn't. I should have drove home to my children, my grandchildren, but I didn't. Through it all, my life somehow always belonged to her. I was selfish for having left her all those years ago, and to send her body out to sea, alone. I owed her. I couldn't shake her. *Haley.* I never could. I should've done anything else, left, ran away, but I didn't.

Instead, I took off my clothes and walked into the cold vast deep that was to become my home.

[23] The Mermaid's Gallows

My feet, at first, sank deep into the wet sand leading into the ocean, but the farther I walked, the more my feet became distanced from the sand and soon I found myself floating in the salty sea instead of drowning. To die, I'd have to push beneath the surface, dive between the crashing waves and force my way into the depths.

Immediately I trembled, realizing only in that moment just how dim the darkness was and how cold the black water was that surrounded me. Panicking, suddenly afraid of my surroundings and the creatures that lurked within [I couldn't for the life of me figure out why, after all, I wanted nothing more in that moment than to die and the creatures could only fail me, nothing worse], I decided it best to swim out farther from the shore, and with every sweep of my arms, I pushed a little more towards the bottom of the black ocean. I came here to die, to find Haley in whatever realm lay beyond this world, but as I came closer to death, I found myself afraid to push on, proving once again to be a coward. Out of rage and frustration with myself, I swam even farther into the murky deep, and the water grew colder with every thrust of my arms, with every kick of my legs, and it wasn't long before I felt as if I was no longer swimming, but floating, or perhaps somehow standing still, in an abyss, what felt like a vacuum, as if I was paused in time, struggling for breath in the void of outer space.

It was time.

When my lips parted to take in a breath of salt water [the taste of death/Haley pushing past my lips, my tongue, and down my throat], I felt the brush of cold flesh against my cheeks as two small hands were placed gently on either side of my face. I opened my eyes and was taken aback at the sight of a beautiful woman, her arms outstretched and embracing me. I wasn't sure if I was more startled at the thought of knowing this woman was here in the water with me, or at the thought of actually seeing her, here in the depths where there was no light [or wasn't before, I should say, as her body seemed to be an actual source of light, emitting a strange greenish glow]. Her skin was translucent, however it was not difficult to make out the smaller details of her body, her form, despite the glow. She was naked and resembled a female human from the waist up, however just below her navel, her skin grew course and plated, as if she had been torn in half and repaired with parts that didn't quite belong. Her legs were not legs at all, but a single tongue of flesh, scaled, with a large fin running off at the end. Her arms appeared to be human-like at first, but upon closer inspection, they too displayed small fins on each forearm, and each had hands attached at the wrists with webbed flesh stretched taut between every one of its ten fingers. She was a mermaid, and quite possibly the most beautiful creature I had ever laid eyes upon.

She didn't say a word, instead she used her hands to pull my face toward hers, parting her lips and placing them directly onto mine. She breathed into me, and I could feel her breath filling my lungs. I exhaled through my nose, and the air escaped in tiny bubbles through my nostrils, racing each other to the surface as if each of them too were alive and dying, anxious to make it to safety. She breathed into me again, and this time I noticed her taste as her tongue slowly crept into my mouth. It was not the same taste as Haley's. Instead of death, I tasted something reminiscent of the ocean itself, salt, the taste of tears. As her tongue pushed its way into my mouth, I took it as a kiss, a gesture of love or perhaps lust, exchanged between two of earth's loveliest creatures. It was beautiful, but quickly I learned it was not what it seemed. Her tongue wrapped around mine and gripped tight, as if inside her mouth there was a small serpent instead of a tongue, strangling its prey. However, it was immediately clear that she had no intention of bringing me bodily harm, as the moment our tongues interlocked, I began receiving messages inside my mind, sent from the mermaid herself, at least that's the simplest way to describe it. She communicated through her tongue, but not in the way humans did. Through her tongue, she connected the nervous systems of our bodies and all at once we had become one being, inside each other's mind, knowing what the other was thinking without having to speak a single word.

The mermaid's thoughts flickered through my mind, as if we were two great computers downloading information into each other. As her past seeped into me, I felt an overwhelming amount of sadness shudder throughout my body. Visions of fishermen on the shore, casting nets and lines, and pulling bodies out of the dark ocean in the hundreds came rushing through my thoughts, as clear as the water that surrounded me. The fishermen were hunting mermaids and filleting the meat from their bones to sell at the market. There was so much blood spilled and running off the boats that the black ocean was temporarily stained bright red, and so was the beach, as the men dragged the skinned and gutted corpses from their boats, out onto the land, and hanged what was left of their bodies with thick rope from the palm trees that ran along the shoreline, including even those too young to scale [not because of any moral reasoning, but because there simply was not enough meat to husk from their underdeveloped bones]. Their bodies swayed in the salty winds rolling off the water, and blood dripped onto the sands below them until the sun grew hot enough to bake the remaining strips of flesh and dry them up. The gulls ate well in those days, some even growing so fat off the putrid flesh they could no longer fly. The gods of the sea had utterly failed the mermaids.

    I opened my eyes and could see depression set deep in the mermaid's eyes, so somber she could have been crying, though in the belly of the ocean it was hard to tell such things. She pushed one final breath into my lungs before unlocking our tongues and pulling away from our embrace. I wondered at that moment what had become of the mermaids, if there were others, or if she was the last of her kind, but before I could make an attempt to speak, she had already scooped me in her arms, and swam swiftly into the darkness with me hooked beneath her, pinned close to her exposed torso and breasts. I closed my eyes and imagined her flesh was Haley's. It took everything in me not to tear off my clothing and press our naked bodies together, not so much in a sexual way, but just to feel close to her in the way that can only be attained through skin-on-skin contact. It was something I often wished I shared with Haley, but our flame went out much too quick, before we ever got the chance to really burn. I controlled my impulses, however, and opened my eyes, trying hard not to stare at the mermaid's exposed breasts, despite them being directly in my line of vision. I was embarrassed of the feelings I felt for this creature, but mostly because I knew they were based on false pretenses. She was not kissing me, after all, only communicating, and the desire to touch her flesh only stemmed from my desire to touch Haley. Nothing more. I pushed these thoughts away at once and turned to face the dark water before me.

The faster and farther into the abyss she swam, the colder the water became, getting so frigid I felt close to hypothermia at times. Every minute or so she would pull my face close to hers and breathe for me again, but only a breath or two at a time, just enough to keep me alive. I would have drowned myself there beneath her, just as I had intended to do when I first walked into the dark water, had I not been curious as to what it was this extraordinary creature wanted to show me. I held myself close to her.

Seeing more than a foot around our swirling bodies, twisting through the currents and secret valleys hidden between large rocks on the ocean floor, was impossible for me, however she seemed to navigate through the dark water without any known trouble. A split second before entering, I was able to make out a sliver of an opening somewhere along the ocean floor, and we swam down into it, our bodies barely slender enough to pass through. Just beyond the slit was a small cave with large slabs of rock jutting out at places along the walls. On each of these slabs lay unconscious mermaids, twelve of them in total, each carrying a glow so dim they almost appeared to be dead at first glance. Once inside, the mermaid pulled me close and wove our tongues together so as to connect our bodies in a way she could communicate with me once again. The instant her salty tongue locked onto mine, visions of the surrounding mermaids appeared to me, but in a different setting.

With my eyes closed and the mermaid's tongue clinched tightly around mine, I could see her thoughts and memories play out in my head like some poorly edited film, jumping back and forth between scenes and timelines, taking in her story and rearranging the details inside my head so they made a little more sense. The story of these thirteen mermaids caused me to feel similar to what I was feeling before

I'd ever stepped into these waters, an overwhelming amount of guilt, but not within me, within the creature embracing me. Out of empathy, I felt compelled to help her, but at first wasn't sure how. In a way, however, she told me.

But first, her story...

Somewhere in the open ocean, twelve lights shuffled just below the water's surface, the lights being the mermaids that were now resting inside the cave surrounding me. Another sat high on a flat rock jutting out above the ocean at a slight angle, enough to rest comfortably atop. This mermaid was the one that saved me, the one that breathed for me, the one that gave me these brilliant visions. She watched as her sisters played together in the shallow part of the ocean, just before the shore, then looked to the sky and admired the clouds hanging above her head. She had always taken interest in wonders outside her world, such as flying creatures in the sky and those that walked upon the land, but was always cautious of man. It wasn't that she felt humans were her enemy necessarily, but she had been around long enough to know when they were around, all they wanted to do was destroy, not just the mermaids, but everything. It was their nature. In a way she felt sorry for them, but pity never drove her to interact with them in any way, well, until now, with her mouth pushed against mine, but even still, this was out of desperation, I'd come to find out, and not out of pity or even because it was typical of her character. It wasn't. She couldn't afford to be careless, none of them could, as they were the last of their kind. Which would explain her panic in the memory as she rolled over on the rock only to see a group of men, about six in total, throwing what looked to be spears with long black leads into the water, in the direction of the twelve glowing mermaids.

Had she been able to scream in that moment, she would have, but mermaids are not equipped to speak. She watched in horror as the men tossed rolled bunches of leads out into the water, then pull-started an engine to which all the leads were attached. In an instant, there was a terrible sound, one that could only be compared to the crack of thunder, and for a split second the water shined bright with bolts of electricity and then disappeared. Another clap of thunder sounded, but this time the sound came from the shore. The engine had backfired, exploded, killing all six of the men instantly. Their bodies lay blackened and bloody on sands of the beach.

She leapt from the rock and dove straight into the ocean, swimming as fast as she could to her sisters' rescue. Each of the twelve mermaids had been knocked unconscious from the electrocution and had since floated to the surface. One by one, she scooped her sisters in her arms and took them to the safest place she'd ever known, the cave in which they lay now. She waited by their side until each of them had regained consciousness, but not a one was ever the same as before, as they had all become completely paralyzed. Of course, this caused great stress within her, as she had all in an instant become the caregiver of all twelve of her sisters, and the last of the dying mermaid race. Each of them deeply wounded and slowly dying, and all she knew to do was to try and keep them from feeling any pain as they made the transformation from life to death, so she kept them drugged.

In the mornings, she'd go hunting for jellyfish and by the afternoon she'd have enough to keep her sisters out of pain throughout the night. I thought of Haley the moment this vision came over me, and how she injected the jellyfish blood into her veins that fateful night all those years ago, and instantly I longed for death again, but could not get myself to break away from the creature at my tongue. I continued watching as the visions flickered inside my mind, and I could see the mermaid injecting her sisters in the same way as Haley injected herself, but being different creatures, their bodies did not reject the jellyfish blood as Haley's did. It kept them out of pain, so she kept up her routine, and years later, there they were, still laying in the same position, the same rocks in the same cave, and she is still hunting and injecting and serving. This became her life. A sort of nurse working inside some mermaid crack house, making sure each of them were doped up just enough to die a little easier, creating a den of mermaid junkies, and in turn giving up her own life to serve them.

And that's when it occurred to me, why I was there, why I was the one human she'd ever come in contact with her entire life. She needed out. They all needed out. She wanted me to put them out of their misery, her included, and would not allow me to die until I had helped them pass on, bringing them out of their wretchedness once and for all. I'd like to think I came up with that on my own, but I'm certain in a strange way the mermaid had communicated her wishes through our connected tongues, though it was hard to tell for sure what thought belonged to whom in the moment.

Regardless, knowing exactly how it feels to live with such grief, I agreed to help her, all of them, though just the thought of bringing myself to kill these creatures was completely terrifying to me. After all, I'd never been one for hunting, and had never killed anything in all my life, so much as an insect, so the thought of killing a creature, especially one that so closely resembled a human, filled me with horror and anxiety of the likes I hadn't before experienced. Had I planned to live afterwards, I don't think I could have ever agreed to do it, however, knowing I would die only minutes after the deed was done, I was able to bring myself up to the task.

I agreed to help and she took me back to the shore where I waited, wet, cold, and alone, for her to return. One by one, she brought each of her sisters to the surface and I helped her by pulling their slack bodies up out of the water and onto the sand. I lined them up side-by-side until all twelve of them were in place and dimly glowing. Studying the grounds that surrounded me, the method of murder came simply out of a lack of options. Never would I have chosen such a violent, inhumane death as a means of euthanasia, but the only tools I could gather there on the shore that brought about a quick, painless death, were the stones that reared from the sands along the coast.

With great hesitation, I held the rock in my hands, hovering above the skull of the first sister. I glanced over to the caregiver and silently sought her approval, some sort of confirmation, a sign that this was indeed what she wanted. She nodded her head, and took her place at the end of the row. I let my fingers slide out from beneath the stone and it fell to the earth, collapsing the sister's skull against the beach. Blood leaked out from beneath the rock, staining the sand a red so dark it almost appeared black. The dim glow of the sister's body left at the exact moment of death. Her nude torso turned a pale grey, and her fin almost black, like a switch had been flipped off within her, changing her outer appearance in an instant.

It took some time finding enough suitable stones for the job [I did not want to use the same stone to crush all their skulls, both out of respect and because I truly didn't think I could finish the job had I seen the mess that became of their faces]. As I found each stone, I'd carry it back to the row of sisters and end another life. With the thirteenth stone, I was surprised to find it was much harder to release than any of the others, even the first. The other sisters were barely there, ghosts trapped in an immovable cage. I was saving them, freeing them of their prison, but not her, not the caregiver. The moment I dropped the twelfth stone, the last of her dying sisters was gone. She was made free, at least that's how I felt at the time. Still, she urged me to continue, to find another rock and finish what I had started, what I had promised.

I struggled for several moments, hovering the rock inches above her head, unable to bring myself to let go, wishing in that moment that she was able to speak, to tell me something that would help me follow through with our deal, but of course she said nothing. Had she not raised her arms and pulled the stone down upon herself, I'm not sure I would have ever let go.

Tremendous guilt and sadness rushed over me the moment I heard the faint, sickening crack of her skull giving way to weight of the stone, and at the sight of what was once her lifeblood gushing out onto the sands. With a single glance at the thirteen mermaid sisters, the last of their kind, dead and lined up on the shore, I felt as if all the pressure that had been weighing on the caregiver had immediately transferred to me, and that, combined with the guilt of Haley, caused me to scream out in such a way I could feel my vocal cords tear from the strain. In an effort to destroy the guilt, the sadness, and the rage born form that, I turned and ran into the salty sea, swimming out as far and as deep as I could, so I could not save myself had I a change of heart, as all cowards did in moments like that.

I was accepted into the water just as prey was welcomed into the mouth of a hunter, and the ocean moved around me and pushed at my back, pulling me in. I wouldn't have been able to run away had I tried. My lips parted and the salty sea entered my mouth, and penetrated my lungs, triggering my gag reflex. I took in more water, vomited it all out, then took it in again, repeating this cycle until my throat grew tired and at last gave up the fight.

But. I. Lived. Through. It. All.

Much to my surprise, drowning did not kill me. Somehow my body was able to take in water and give up oxygen without killing me instantly...or at all. Instead, my body sank to the bottom of the ocean, straight into the mouth of the mermaid den I had just been inside something like an hour before. I discovered this, in what must have been several days later, only after an anglerfish had wandered in through the opening of the cave, displaying a faint light on the end of a biological rod sticking outward off the front of its face. Because of the way the dim light illuminated its grotesque face, with its beady soulless eyes and cartoonish horrid mouth, at first I thought it to be a devil, some hellish creature meant to take my soul away at the precise moment of death, assuming it too had become lost in the dark waters, just as I had, and was only now catching up with me. After days of weeping on the freezing stone floor of the ocean, tears of terror, guilt, and frustration melding with the surrounding water, I wished the vision of this devil to be true. I wanted nothing more in that moment than for it to reach out and rip my soul apart. I was beyond tired of living, past the point of suicide, and death would have been the sweetest relief—the *only* relief—I could have received, however the vision was not true. Swimming before me was a simple creature of the earth, and the only joy it brought me was its natural ability to illuminate my surroundings.

    I took the creature in my arms and explored the depths, finding a handful of syringes filled with jellyfish blood, the drugs the mermaids had yet to use before having been put out of their misery. Holding the syringes immediately put me in mind of Haley, opening her serpent box while sitting on the sand, and how she used the jellyfish blood to slip easily into death. That's when I slid the needle into the crook of my arm, hoping this was the reason I was unable to die, as if drowning was not poetic enough, or perhaps it simply was not the death I deserved. I felt a slight pinch at first, then with the push of the plunger I felt nothing at all. For a moment I was convinced I died there on the ocean floor, as all feelings of pain and guilt immediately left my body, but the drug soon wore off and the pain became all too real again.

I spent the next couple weeks pushing the contents of the syringes into my veins until every last one of them was emptied inside me. The jellyfish blood did not bring pleasure of any kind, only temporary relief— numbness. I was meant to live with the guilt, that much was painfully clear. I could not be killed, no matter the method or how often I tried. I could have kept going. I could have refilled the syringes with more blood and kept slipping into tiny comas at the bottom of the sea, but I realized at that point I would be no longer doing it with the hope of dying, only to remain numb, and that was the coward's way out. If I were to accomplish anything in life, it would be to squash the coward that lived within me. I could not let it define me. I could only be defined by Haley's death, by my shattered heart brought on by unrequited love, true love, and the consequences of choosing to live all those years without her.

So I swam back to the shore, emptying the salt water from my lungs, stinging my throat as it all came gushing out of me. I found it particularly cruel that God, or whatever it was keeping me alive through all this, would not allow me to die, but still allow me to feel pain. Well, I thought it cruel then, but as the years passed on from that moment, I learned to appreciate the pain. In fact, I even came to *enjoy* the pain. It may sound odd, but being immune to death sometimes made me feel as if I weren't alive at all, that life was what was happening all around me and I was nothing more than a pitiful being that somehow still physically existed even though I had died inside many years ago. The pain kept me in check. It reminded me I was still alive, and more than that, it reminded me that I was still being punished, over Haley, over choosing life over love, over the mermaids—the thirteen sisters of the dark water and the last of their kind. I became their gallows. Cancer became mine, or so I had hoped. Only time would tell.

Remember, only those of us who have been shitty people in life become thrilled with an honorable exit, no matter how vile, just as this terrible, hopeless disease would bring.

My vision weakened and left me long ago. In the last moments of sight, I was surrounded by machines in some hospital, and my daughter was weeping at my side. I remember her reaching for my hand, though my hand was no longer there, no longer part of me. Instead, she caressed thick scar tissue at the end of a blackened stump that was somehow my arm. My hands, along with at least half of the rest of my body, had died and was removed surgically to prevent the gangrene from spreading any farther. This was not my decision, of course, as I would have welcomed the death into my body gladly. The doctors, along with my family, were trying to save me, or at least trying to prevent me from dying in ways worse than cancer itself. I would have told them not to bother, to let the sickness spread until all that was left of me was some sort of decayed biological soup, but many parts of me simply just did not work anymore, including my mouth, so I was unable to communicate my wishes in any way whatsoever.

I imagine I've become hideous to gaze upon. By now, I should've become a true terror, a nightmare vision made flesh, worthy of an entire chapter in one of those dense medical textbooks, and certainly in one of those books about freaks. Perhaps I'd be the subject of a chapter titled "Queen of the Freaks," or "World's Greatest Anomaly." I'd wear that honor proudly, as I shall one day be no more than a skinless torso, a blackened heart beating inside an otherwise empty ribcage, along with a severed spinal cord with a gray, shrunken, tumor-filled brain hanging limply atop. That should be me. That should be what I become.

And still I'll be changing even more with every day that passes. I will continue to decompose until the ugliness of my outer appearance matches the ugliness that is inside my terrible, selfish heart.

And. I. Will. Live. Through. It. All.

Until my existence becomes only a low humming of static. It's how I'll know I'm still alive.

[static]

[32] If You Don't Sleep, You Don't Dream.

I was hesitant at first to come back to Adam, as I'm not completely comfortable knowing I'm eager to see how the rest of his life unfolds. I feel like a masochist and often wonder if I've always been one or if this damn dial has created that within me. Either way, it feels undeniable. I want to know more of his story, even though watching never fails to bring a great deal of suffering to us both...

VI

I am drawn to the bright lights of a gas station convenience store, much like a moth to flame.
Surrounded by such awful darkness, my breath is short.
I'm growing tired.

Inside the store, I collect a variety of caffeinated products:
pills, energy drinks, coffee.
I can feel the spying eyes of the cashier clerk like hot breath on my neck.
Why has this hideous beast come into my store? he is thinking.

What business does it have here?

My stomach is empty.
I crave a hot meal, but settle for a bag of beef jerky.
The clerk refuses to look at my face
[my grotesque, malformed face].
Even at the counter, as I'm presenting my purchases, he turns away from me.

That'll be five dollars.

Five dollars?

I ask with some confusion.
The jerky alone is more than five dollars.

Five dollars.

But—

Goddamn it, just get out of my store, you wretch!

I pull out my wallet.

This wallet hasn't been open since Gordon found me…
nearly 28 years ago.
I pull out an old twenty and place it on the countertop.
As I gather my purchases, I notice a rack of maps by the doorway.
I take a city map on my way out the door.

Out on the street, I take a handful of caffeine pills and wash them down with hot black coffee.
I walk the wet city streets until I find a park bench on which to rest.
I unfold the map.
Gordon's note only consisted of seven words:
I will wait for you in Hell.

In Hell…
I remember a time when Gordon took me to a place called Hell.
It wasn't the same Hell from the bible, but He still called it that all the same.
This place was underground.

Yes! I remember!
Poseidon!
Dig, dig, dig!

Steen!
I look at the map, frantically searching for the words
Poseidon and Steen.
I trace every street with the tip of my finger, finding nothing.

A droplet of rain taps and soaks into the map.
Tap... tap, tap... tap.
I fold the map and tuck it into my pocket.
I need to find shelter.

Across the street, I spot an electronics store.
TVs glow brilliantly in the front window display.
In the alleyway next to the store, I spot several large empty cardboard boxes.
I turn one over and slip inside.
Settling into my home for the evening, I grab a day old newspaper from the trash bin and crack open an energy drink.

Thirty minutes later, despite the copious amounts caffeine tripping through my bloodstream, I fall fast asleep.

VII

The brightness of the room burns out my eyes, closed lids and all.
I can hear rustling coming from somewhere nearby.
Blindness fades as the light slowly dims, allowing me to open my eyes.
The room is large with tall ceilings.
The floor is nonexistent.
Only dirt lay beneath my feet.
Hanging from the ceiling are a thousand light bulbs, burning dim.
I walk slowly through the sea of electric glass, searching for the origin of the rustling.
I search until I am face-to-face with it.

It's Gordon, but He has changed.
Many of His bones are exposed through tears in His skin.
Half His face is mechanized.
Sparks shower through His teeth instead of speech.
His grin is permanently fixed through gashes in His cheeks.

I am dreaming again.

Gordon pays me no mind.
His attention is directed at the ground below.
He drills His left hand into the soil, scooping what He can into His hands and forming the collected dirt into a packed ball.
He takes a bite as if it were an apple.
He swallows and looks up at me.
His seriousness panics me.

He takes another bite of His dirt apple and the room steadily becomes darker.

> *Death is simple, my son. It is life that is Hell.*
> *But Hell is what you make it, Laz.*
> *You do not have to suffer.*
> *You do not have to be in pain.*
> *I've taken the pain from your Hell before,*
> *I can do it again.*
> *I can free your mind, Lazarus.*
> *Come to me.*

I walk toward Him.
Once I'm close enough, He grabs me firmly at the neck.

> *All you have to do is give it to them!*
> *Give them your mind!*

Gordon points to two figures in the distance.
Hulking white beasts, they are.
Brutes.
They whip their long-lashing tongues, swallowing light bulbs.
The broken glass gashes their tongues and blood gushes from their mouths like heavy syrup, spattering across the chests of their otherwise perfect, colorless bodies.
As they approach me, I'm able to make out finer details.
They only have one eye, located on the left side of their heads, so they must turn to see where they're going.

As each light bulb is ingested, the room becomes increasingly darker.
The two creatures separate and stampede through the glass.
It's getting dark, dark, dark.
I'm hardly able to see them now.

I try to break free from Gordon's grasp, but struggling only seems to make Him stronger.

They are close now.
Gordon forces me to the ground.

> *Lazarus! You will be born again!*
> *Just give it to them!*
> *Give them your mind!*

One of the beasts wraps its slimy tongue around my ankles and pulls my feet into its maw.
It gnaws.
I feel everything as I fill the spaces between its teeth.
Skin is pressed so tight it splits.
Bones shatter.
Blood becomes the mighty river from which the beast drinks.
The pain is excruciating.

Gordon will *not* set me free.

The beast pulls me farther down its throat, till I'm waist deep.
I beat my fists into the crown of the brute and discover it is surprisingly soft.
The thing has no skull.

I dig my crooked fingers into its scalp, ripping the skin apart like a jelly-filled balloon, exposing its wet insides.
The beast squeals in pain, but continues to swallow me.
I push my fingers through its brains and rip away handfuls of meat until its stiletto teeth, now at my chest, cease mastication
and the creature falls into death.

Gordon loosens His grasp.
That's when I notice the other brute is devouring Him.
He is speaking in tongues.

Tk tk tk! Shelz bun on lititio!
Shelz! Shelz! Tk tk tk!

The brute has swallowed all but Gordon's screaming head.
Gordon turns toward me.

It hides from which it spews!
Never forget the persecutor of O—

The brute crushes Gordon's yipping skull with a final bite.

Blood, brains, and bits of bone ooze through its wicked teeth.

When I finally awaken from my terrible dream, I find I'm still inside the cardboard box, down the alley beside the
electronics shop.
It's damp and the cardboard is collapsing on top of me.
Outside it's still dark, still raining.

VIII

The sweet taste of rat meat absorbs into my taste buds and causes me to salivate like a wild dog.
There isn't much else to eat here on the streets and the jerky didn't last but a few hours.
In the last few days, I've adjusted to the pungent taste of rodent meat.
Truth be told, I've more than just adjusted, I've actually *acquired* the taste.
Sometimes a rat will cross my path and I will snap its neck and suck the meat off its bones, even without the need...
without hunger.

I like how the taste lingers on my tongue long after it's gone down.
So much so I don't think I'd ever *not* want to taste it.
The succulent juices should coat my lips...always.

Lucky for me, there are plenty of rats in this town.

I've been cautious in the ways I travel: walking the streets by night, and covering my face with a scarf and resting by day.
I've walked the many streets of this city ten times over looking for any signs of familiarity, but have found nothing.

Then something catches my eye.

A woman.
A young woman, maybe thirty years old.
She is buried somewhere behind two heavy scarlet curtains hanging in a window.
I am only able to see her through an opening between the two curtains, no more than an inch wide.
She is sitting on her bed, completely nude, painting her toenails.

Her toenails and her lips are as red as the curtains hanging between us.
After she finishes, she turns on her side [facing me] and falls asleep.
I stand at her window for nearly six hours, just watching her breathe and studying the contours of her perfect body.

Something inside me stirs.

I fall in love. I have to have her. She is mine!

Now, I am no dreamer.
I don't expect anything to come of this.
I don't ever plan to approach her with these feelings.
I know I'm nothing but scarred skin above and old bones beneath.
Still, something inside me wants to watch over her.
I want to be there for her if ever there is a need.

So that's what I do.
I follow her.
I follow her to her work [The Corner Diner].
I follow her shopping.

I watch as she meets a group of friends for drinks and even help her to her door when she is too drunk to walk.
She does not remember when I do.

She even saves me from my dreams!
Rarely now do I ever dream of Gordon!
Most of my dreams revolve around the night I first saw her.

I lose track of her and decide to fall asleep just to dream of her.
I awaken with a fierce hunger.
I swallow the last bit of rat meat and pitch the bones into a nearby dumpster.

It's sunset.
She should be home by now.

Walking the street to her house, I notice an unfamiliar vehicle parked in her driveway.
My suspicions fuel as I hear her scream!
I run to her window and look through the opening between the curtains.
There is a man.
He is hurting her.
I run to the door and kick it in.

The man looks over at me.

> GET OFF OF... HER!

> *Who the fuck are you?*

I run over and pull the man off of her.
The woman screams at the sight of me.
Such a beast!
Such a hideous, monstrous beast, I am!
The man, much stronger and younger than I,
plants his fist into my face, sending me
straight to the floor.
He picks me up and rears his fist back,
wanting to hit me again.

> *Wait! David... STOP!*

The woman screams.
I'm slowly losing consciousness in his grasp.

> *It's my father!*

IX

Shadow people surround me.
Their eyes and mouths glow red electricity.
I can feel the vibrations of their speech.
The shadow people fade and become real
people: doctors, nurses.
I'm tied to a gurney and they're pushing me
down a long hospital hallway.
One of the nurses places an oxygen mask over
my nose and mouth.

The shadows return and the mask becomes a
muzzle.
I thrash about trying to free myself from my
restraints.
One of the electric mouths speaks.

Hold his head down!
He will be out any second now.

The shadows once again fade and I'm able to
see the woman from the window [my
daughter?] walking at my side.
Mascara is streaked down her cheeks from
tears.

The shadows cloud and blind me once again.

*The sedative is kicking in, doctor.
He should be out within the minute.*

And then there was peace.

X

A woman speaks, wrapping her arms tightly around my waist.

*Look at them, Adam...
I've never seen them so happy.*

I'm suddenly a younger man standing at the edge of the world looking out at the vast sea.
The salty breeze combs through my hair and I am free.
Two children, a boy and a girl, are playing in the sand.
Their laughter warms my heart.
We watch as the children take turns burying each other in the sand.

Ah, to feel such life again!

Sadly, the moment is short-lived.

I'm back in the hospital room and it is slightly larger than the one I stayed in before…and more decorative.
Images of familiar faces stare at me from all angles of the room, hanging in tiny glass frames.
I stare at the photos trying to remember a name…*anything.*

A doctor and a nurse enter the room and disrupt my thoughts.
The nurse begins her routine of checking my vitals without even acknowledging my consciousness.
The doctor studies and writes on his clipboard, also seemingly ignoring me.

Lazarus…

The doctor speaks.
His eyes still focused on his clipboard.

I hadn't noticed before, but the door is iron
and the windows are barred.

> *Where do I begin?*
> *Well, as you've probably*
> *noticed, your room is...*
> *more or less, a prison cell.*
> *You've been placed under arrest*
> *on suspicion of multiple rape charges.*
> *It turns out the semen sample*
> *we took during your first visit*
> *Matched samples taken from several rape victims*
> *linked with the case against Gordon.*

This hardly comes as a shock, given the
nightmares I've been having lately.
Still, the very thought of being capable of
such a heinous crime makes my stomach turn.
Forever a nasty beast, I am.

The nurse pretends not to hear any of this.
She puts away her instruments and leaves the
room as quickly as she can.
She is nervous.
Terrified.
Of me.

> And I am not in prison?

*Well, the police feel it is necessary to continue testing...
especially the dream studies.*

It is clear I'm their only link to Gordon.
Such fools!
Gordon can never be captured or contained.
Gordon has created flesh! LIFE!
Such a God cannot be defeated by mere men.

*We had a discussion with the young
lady who brought you in...
your daughter, Joan.
She told us your real name is
Adam Argyl.
It seems to us, the medical staff,
that Gordon has given you the
nickname 'Lazarus' as a reference
to the biblical tale of Lazarus,
the man who was given a second life.*

This man is a doctor?
Such an obvious "discovery."

*Also, during your last stay
you experienced a perplexing seizure
fit that came as a direct result from a self-injected dose*

of an unknown chemical.

Happiness.

The doctor pauses, puzzled.
He scribbles something down on his clipboard.

Happiness?

That's the name of the chemical.

Oh?

Well, we've discovered that 'happiness' was created to keep your body from rejecting the 'spider implant' we found in your frontal lobe. It created a certain sense of euphoria, am I right?

Euphoria?
Yes, I guess so.

Again, he writes.

> *However, when you last took this 'happiness' drug,*
> *it was after the spider implant had been removed.*
> *This is why your body rejected the chemical.*

Silence now.

> *Do you have any questions?*

I am the one who should be asking this,
not him.

> Absolutely not.

> *Okay then.*
> *In about an hour,*
> *we'll be putting you to sleep to begin testing.*
> *Just ring the nurse if you need anything before then.*

The doctor exits the room.
I sit up on the side of my bed and pull myself
to stand.
The floor is cold against my bare feet.
As I make my way toward the window, the
tubing of my IV gets snagged on the bed,
tearing my skin.

I curse the needle and rip it from my hand.
I open the window and stick my bleeding hand through the bars.
It's still raining.

This goddamn world.

[14] DEMOLITION YA YA

For weeks after the installation of the dial, every time I'd tune in to channel fourteen all I would see was a lone phone booth in the middle of a desert. No matter how long I'd watch, that's all I'd ever see. It wasn't until the phone started ringing that the following visions came...

1.

Unconscious. The heat from the sun licked at my face, blistering flesh with every lash of its fiery whip. Lying flat with the horizon, my back was flat against the hot white sands of the desert, and the heat grew so intense my flesh bubbled despite being protected by a thick red leather jacket. By the time I awakened, my body had cooked for so long that the whole goddamn desert smelled like a porterhouse. The aroma found its way into my nostrils, instantly awakening my senses. My eyes opened and rolled back into my head, screaming back at the daylight. More than just cooked, my body was beaten, bloody, and bruised. There was a hole in my right cheek two inches wide that was leaking blood like a running faucet. Blood also trickled out from the inside of my ears, drying into a flaky crust against my red, sunburned skin. My tongue, dry as sandpaper, painfully pressed and spread apart my cracked scabbed lips. I struggled to pull myself to a sitting position. As I did, I noticed the white v-neck t-shirt I was wearing was stained with a concoction that looked to be two parts blood, one part motor oil. *Who's blood?* I wasn't sure.

A small vibration trembled along the sand. I cupped my hands over my eyes like a visor and looked out into the distance. The vision of a silver semi-truck appeared and fizzled away almost immediately, wavering in the heat, as if it was only a hallucination. I pushed up to my feet. The palms of my hands were protected from the scalding sands by thick black leather biker gloves with the fingers cut out. The topside of the gloves sported a patch of mirrored metal studs that shined like a fist of diamonds under the sun. I stood and stretched, but quickly buckled over from a sharp pain piercing through my stomach. I wrapped both arms around my abdomen and howled, feeling as if I'd just been stabbed in the gut with hot piece of sharp metal.

The low hum of the truck's engine grew louder as it drew closer. I had to suck up the pain and get moving if I was going to get to the road in time to catch it. I closed my eyes and took a deep breath before hobbling towards it. I came within ten feet of my destination before my joints gave out and I collapsed to the ground, as if in that moment a syringe was stuck into my neck containing just enough poison to paralyze me. The sand immediately resumed cooking my skin, sizzling, and it was then that I noticed the vultures swarming over me, like dark angels of death, waiting for me to slip into unconsciousness so they could pick the meat clean from my bones. *The pain in my stomach. The hole in my face.* Guess they jumped the gun. Had they waited just a few minutes longer to begin their feast, I likely never would have woken up.

Lucky me. *Ha, right.*

The truck's rattle grew louder, passing me and then faded away again. The birds dropped from the sky, almost in unison, afraid one would get a mouthful more than the others. They creeped along the sand cautiously, and drew nearer with every step. I was too weak to put up a fight, so I just stared into their soulless black eyes for as long as I could, which proved to be only a few short seconds. I remembered thinking their faces looked odd, unlike any other bird I was familiar with. It was as if their faces had all been turned inside-out. Like they weren't even of the earth, but instead some demon fowl spawned in the deepest circle of Hell. Then my eyes closed.

A few seconds later, a drum-piercing squeal forced my eyelids open, and the vultures took to the sky again. The truck driver was braking. The stench of burnt tire rubber polluted the air as the truck was thrown into reverse.

2.

The driver stopped for gas an hour or so down the road. We didn't talk much, as I discovered I didn't know anything at all about what I was doing out in the desert, and that was the only question he ever asked me. Guess he figured I wasn't much for talking and left it at that. Truth be told, I wasn't even sure myself if I was much of a talker, as I wasn't aware of my own identity. As far I figured, I was born right there on the sand, just moments before he picked me up. I wondered if I was even meant to be anything at all. Perhaps I was molded and placed in the world by God himself as a way to feed the vultures. Maybe that's how it all worked: God intervened and things survived. These thoughts got me wondering if I was a religious man, before the desert, if I had even *existed* before the desert, that is. When the driver stopped, I took a look at the fuel gauge and saw the tank was three-quarters full. He pulled up to the tank and nodded at the door, silently asking me to exit. He was ditching me. I nodded back, thanked him, and opened the door.

Across the street was a small diner. I wasn't sure how long it had been since I'd eaten anything, but I felt close to starving, so I headed over. As I entered, I must have been quite the sight, cause just about every damned person in the building stopped eating and stared at me. The whole place had gone silent in an instant, except for the murmuring of a news anchorman coming from a television hanging in the far corner of the room. I wasn't offended by their stares. I'd yet to see the bubbled-gore that had become of my flesh, but

I could damn sure feel it. I didn't blame them for staring. Hell, I'd be staring too if it weren't *my* scorched hide walking through the door.

I weaved through the sea of gawking eyes, hobbling back towards the door into the kitchen. Inside, there was a teenage boy washing dishes in the sink. He caught a glimpse of me and pulled a butcher knife out from the water, pointing it at me and backing away slowly. I paid him no mind. The pain I was feeling in that moment was so excruciating that being stabbed really wouldn't have made much of a difference. My fingers were so burnt and blistered that I had trouble turning the knobs on the faucet. After seeing I wasn't there to bring trouble, the boy let the knife drop to his side and turned the faucet on for me. I cupped my hands under the stream and drank the cool water that pooled inside.

3.

I took a seat at the breakfast bar. When the waitress came around, I ordered only a single piece of toast. It was the only word I could manage to mutter in the moment, *toast*. Later, I realized the irony. Carefully, I removed my studded leather gloves, which were serving no real purpose indoors, except to agitate my burned skin. I examined the defined line on my flesh where my red, blistered fingers met the pale white of my palms.

The waitress returned with the toast, pulled the bill from her apron and tore it up.

"It's on the house, hun. You take it easy, you hear?" the waitress said, then smiled at me. I did my best to smile back.

Something crawled out from underneath the toast and walked out onto the countertop. It was an insect. A small black cricket. The waitress sighed and smashed it violently against the countertop with a spoon. Yellow insect guts spurted out from beneath the utensil as its armored skin popped and split apart from the weight crushing down upon it.

"Goddamn crickets. They're bad this year," she said, wiping the spoon off on her apron before returning it to its place next to my plate. I wasn't bothered by it. I wouldn't have used it anyway.

I reached around and tugged on the sleeve of my jacket. It took a solid minute, but I managed to remove the jacket completely. The cool air prickled against my sunburned flesh and almost instantly dried the layer of sweat that covered my arms and back. The feeling it brought was a nice contrast to the pain.

As I picked up the toast, I noticed something written on my forearm in heavy black ink: PINKY—(859) 279-8094.

4.

I scanned my thoughts for any trace of the name *Pinky*. Sun, dehydration, and blood loss was a dangerous combination that proved to be not so good on the memory. Hell, I wasn't even sure who I was myself, let alone this *Pinky* person.

I had to call the number.

I reached into my pocket and pulled out a wad of cash—easily $10,000, all in one hundred dollar bills. Seeing this much money in my hands was surprising, but it was still second on my mind to the mysterious name written on my arm. I decided it best to push the wad of bills back into my pocket and explore more on that later, but not before leaving a hundred on the countertop as a tip for the waitress. I stood and folded the jacket over my arm and tucked the gloves inside one of the pockets. The people sitting at the tables around me continued to stare at me, some were even whispering to each other.

As I exited the diner, a voice behind me shouted, "Give 'em hell, McKenna!"

I looked back for only a second, then nodded and walked out the door.

5.

Just outside the diner, there stood a small rack of brochures, all of them advertising popular Texas locales. I picked up a brochure with the word DESCARTES written across the top and unfolded it, studying the map on the inside. *Texas?* Nothing looked familiar to me. I traced my fingers along the map, looking for any clue of my exact location.

Reading the names of the surrounding areas seemed to jog my memory a bit. Information flickered rapidly inside my mind, but left me before I could comprehend any of it. I folded the map and stared at the brochure's cover. DESCARTES. The word was written in all capitals, as if it was screaming at me from the page, demanding my attention and commanding to be remembered. There was a reason I picked up this brochure, I was certain of it. I must have known this place. Somehow it seemed significant. I folded the brochure in half again and tucked it into the back pocket of my jeans. *Maybe it would come to me later*, I thought, then went to find a pay phone.

6.

[phone ringing]

Hello?

Eh...Pink-ee?

Finn? Oh my god, Finn, is that you?

. . .

Everyone's looking for you! Jesus. Where the hell have you been?

Uh, Pinky...I'm hurt...bad.

What do you mean, hurt? How bad?

Bad.

How bad is bad?

I look like a...a deep fried...hot dog.

*Hot dog? Christ, Finny, we've gotta get
you out of this shit.
This year is it. No more. You win and
we go back to Colorado.
No more of this Demolition Ya Ya shit.
You're going to get yourself killed.*

Colorado?

Jesus, Finny, what the hell is wrong with you?

I'm not feeling well. Can't think straight.

When are you coming to get me?

. . .

Finn, I can't take it much longer.

*I know you wanted me to keep low,
at least until you got the brutes off your back,
but damn, honey, it's been three days now.
When are you going to come get me?*

The brutes?

You shook them, didn't you? Didn't you?!

. . .

*Tell me you're at least using a secure line
to make this call?*

Pinky, I'm sorry...I don't know.
I don't know what's goin—

Goddamn it, Finn! Are you being serious right now?

I told you, I'm not feeling so great.
I don't remember...anything.

*You killed me, Finny! You fucking killed me!
I knew better than to get mixed up
with Finn McKenna!
Why the hell—*

[cut]

[static]

7.

The line was dead. My first thought was that it was cut from her end, but once I went to hang up the receiver I noticed it was my phone cord that had been severed. I turned around to find three of the most grisly men in I'd ever seen, real bottom-of-the-barrel-type guys. They cornered me inside the phone booth by blocking my only exit. One of them was spinning a pocketknife in his hand.

"Well, well, well, boys...lookie what we gots here," the man with the knife said, smiling. "If'n it ain't Finn McKenna himself. What the fuck happened to you, boy? Some feller stick you in the microwave too long?" The men snickered. The smell of whiskey clouded around them.

On the phone, Pinky mentioned shaking the 'brutes.' I wondered if these men were the ones she was referring to. These guys were bad news for sure, but *brutes?* No, couldn't be. The name suggested something larger, something more...*grotesque*. But still, I asked.

"Are you guys...*brutes?*" my gravel-rasp voice leaked.

The men looked shocked at first, and then busted out in laughter. The one with the knife put his arm around me and slapped me on the back.

"Shit, boy, they did you in good, huh? Fucked yer brain all up." I noticed the man was squinting, as if he was trying to look inside my ear, all the way to my brain. "I bet that brain of yers is like a fucking fried egg," the man said, and continued to stare in silence.

After a few moments passed, the man broke his stare and said, "Naw, we ain't no brutes. We's just men, like yourself, lookin' to get us a slice of that Demolition Ya Ya pie."

"Demolition Ya Ya?" *Those words again.*

"Holy shit! It's gonna be easy as hell to get this fuck. He don't even know the damn game he's playin'," the man with the knife said, positioning the blade in such a way that the sun reflected into my eyes.

"Could be puttin' us on," one of the other men finally spoke up. He looked at me with a suspicious eye. "Y'know...tryin' to catch us off guard."

"C'mon, now, just look at the poor bastard," the man with the knife said. "His skin's done melted clear off the bone. His brain's been bar-be-que'd! If'n you gets in real close, you can even smell him. He's cooked a good medium-well!"

I shook the man's arm off my shoulder. His face was flushed with anger. He grabbed my neck and held the knife up to my teeth.

"Now, I may not be no fuckin' brute, but by god, I can *kill* a man. Now I suggest you be on your best behavior from now on, cause I can go with the *money*...or I can go with *guttin' ya*. Don't really make no difference to me. Either way, I leave happy."

"What money?" I asked.

"Shit, boy. You knock something retarded in there?"

"Yeah, anyone who turns in a renegade runner from Demolition Ya Ya gets $5,000, paid in cash, everyone knows that!" said one of the other men, the one with a long scar running across his cheek. "Figure us boys could split it three ways."

The man with the knife clinched his jaw and punched Scarface square in the nose with his knife-packed fist.

"Now why the hell d'you go an' say that?"

"What, it's true?" the man said, feeling for any blood that that may have been trickling out of his nostrils.

"I know it's true! Don' mean you should tell it! McKenna's clearly brain-fucked! Let's have a lil' fun with him, shall we?"

"But you were the one who mentioned the money first," Scarface said.

"Goddamn it, I said let's have fun with him. Stop talkin' about the money," the man with the knife said, then pushed the blade against my cheek.

I couldn't take it anymore. I was getting angry. I squeezed my fists together, packing my bones as tight as they'd pack and it caused me to feel something inside I hadn't noticed before, some sort of *rage* building within. Suddenly I felt strong, powerful, and for the first time since I regained consciousness, I felt...*electric*.

8.

The chill-whip lash of the southern desert breeze was cold enough to welt skin, had there been any skin around for it to welt, that is. In this particular part of Texas, a nothing stretch of scorched earth called Peligro, not a single soul was around to experience the unique darkness this part of the earth seemed bring at night. The night in Peligro was black, not dim, not dark, at least not in the way most people experience dark in their towns. Not even the stars dared peek out their heads here. The only light in Peligro came from a solitary streetlamp, oddly enough, considering there wasn't a road anywhere for at least forty miles in all directions. Even stranger, showered in the dim amber glow of the streetlamp was a busted-up telephone booth, covered with meaningless graffiti and the windows all broken. The shattered glass glitter-sparkled on the ground outside the phone booth as if the dirt was fertile with imperfect diamonds. The sight was almost beautiful at a distance.

Tearing into the silence, the phone rang. The vibration from the ring instantly caused a hundred twitching insect legs to convulse and flitter out from the holes of the ear and mouthpieces of the telephone receiver.

The call would not be answered tonight.

9.

As I bandaged my wounds, I examined my hand and discovered I was melting. What I initially thought was scorched flesh now appeared to be a little worse than just that. I was melting, no doubt about it. The skin around each of the fingers on my left hand was welding together, and my hand had started to resemble a fin, like some fucking fish. I thought about my name: Finn McKenna. *Had it always been Finn? Was it a nickname? Was it possible I had had this fin hand all along?*

I then thought about the reaction of people I'd come in contact with since waking up in the desert. Most everyone seemed to recognize me, in this form, melting flesh and everything, which got me thinking I must have been melting for a long time before ever burning in the desert. But those scummy guys, what they said to me... I had to find out more about Demolition Ya Ya. Clearly I was caught in the middle of whatever it was. My mind was a tangled knot of information, and I couldn't shake any of it loose. However, I did manage to remember the stand of brochures outside the diner. I couldn't recall any of the pamphlets mentioning Demolition Ya Ya, but it was worth a shot to go back and check it out.

I had to untie my knots.

I looked at the sky. There was an electrical storm in the distance, heading straight towards the town. For some reason I felt nervous watching the sky as it flickered with bright bolts of electricity, lighting the purple sky a pale pink, then returning again. It was as if my body knew something my mind didn't. I felt an overwhelming urge to take shelter.

I buried my fin hand inside my pocket and headed back to the diner.

10.

I skimmed over the plethora of brochures, looking for any mention of Demolition Ya Ya. No luck. However, one brochure did catch my attention. The front displayed a cityscape, with mammoth buildings towering over oceans of people like gods in the form of architecture. One of the buildings was mirrored, reflecting the dark purple sky and appearing almost totally invisible in the photograph. I opened the brochure and found the building belonged to a company called DangerCom—*"Home of Demolition Ya Ya."* I closed the pamphlet. The cover read: LYKOI.

A faint knocking sound came from somewhere behind me. I turned around and was greeted by the many patrons inside the diner, all pressed up against the large glass windows. Most were looking up at the sky, though some of them were looking at me, pointing upwards, as if trying to warn me of something. I looked up at the sky, but it was too late. Before I even realized I was in danger, a bolt of pink lightning sliced through the air and immediately took hold of my bones. The electricity absorbed into my body, causing my muscles to stiffen, and once the light faded I fell limp to the ground. Smoke rolled off my body in giant belches.

11.

Waking was not easy. A nightmare pranced around inside my skull, gripping my subconscious in such a way it felt as if it were pinching it off and releasing it again, like some sort of water hose of vitality. It did this repeatedly throughout my slumber.

In the nightmare, a hulk of a beast was standing at the feet of a young lady who was sleeping oddly on a marble platform. I say oddly because she didn't seem to be resting comfortably, with her legs folded and turned to the side and her back flat against the platform. It appeared as if she had been heavily sedated and was tossed onto the bed of rock, remaining unconscious and unmoving throughout the entire ordeal. She had not a single shred of clothing on her body. A tattoo of a pink crescent moon wrapped around her right areola and seemed to silently shout at me, demanding my focus, as if to say: *this means something. Pay attention.*

The hulk stood silent, chest heaving, as though out of breath, but eerily no sound was produced through all its huffing. The only sound in the room was the calm whimpering of the woman's terrified unconscious mind, blanketed under her bated breath. The beast slid its fingers across the flesh of her foot, from the toes back, and continued to trace the outline of her leg until it reached her knee. Slowly, it parted her legs until one was on either side of her, sprawled out on the slab like some lifeless bullfrog prepared for dissection. The thing hovering over her had no hue to its skin, well perhaps a hint of white, however translucent, and upon its head there was absolutely no hint of a face, save for two pinhole nostrils and a single eye on the side of its head. I was unable to read its emotions, except through its actions.

With one hand gripped tightly around one of her ankles, the thing reached down between its own legs and stroked its dangling flaccid penis, using its plump fingers, complete with broken, blackened fingernails, to pull back its foreskin, revealing the pale blue bulbous glans hidden underneath. Its chest heaved more rapidly now, but still produced no sound. The beast was aroused, and its cock had grown to be as long and wide as the woman's full torso. The thing pressed its blue meaty bulb against the hammy lips lining the outside of her vagina. Her insides were much too compact for the throbbing beast knocking at its door. It struggled to push its way in. All the while, the woman remained completely unaware any of this was even happening. The warmth of her body caused the blood in the brute's veins to swell and throb, to the point it was almost painful. It began to stroke itself over her, daydreaming of her wet pink insides. It let loose of her ankle and reached up at her face. It pushed one of its fat fingers into her mouth and traced the grooves of her teeth. They each felt tiny and precious against the ends of its sausage-like digits. It rubbed the flesh of its finger over her front teeth, gently massaging the soft, wetness of her gums. The brute's body throbbed with pleasure.

Little flitters of light appeared in the darkness that surrounded them. They revealed themselves to be smaller, malnourished versions of the hulk. They made their way over to the girl, grabbed her at every limb, and pinned her down flat against the platform. At this point, the girl finally awakened and screamed out in pure horror as the hulk pushed its weight down against her legs and forced itself inside her. Even though it only managed to get partway inside, it was still far too much for the woman to handle and she howled out in pain, as if she was giving birth to a full-sized human man, or I suppose just the opposite—more like if a full-sized man was crawling inside of her, a birth reversal. One of the smaller creeps attempted to silence her by jamming its fingers down her throat, while another fondled her full, luscious breasts and bit at her side, causing tiny blood vessels to break and rise to the surface of her skin. The hulk pushed more of its shaft inside her, stretching the opening of her vagina until it split at both the top and bottom, ripping clear through her asshole and all the way up past the patch of hair on her pubic mound. Her muffled screams were barely audible over the freakish laughter of the creeps. The hulk struggled to push itself any farther inside her, but it didn't deter it. It pushed on. A couple of creeps dug their bony fingers beneath the splitting flesh of her vagina and tugged violently at it, tearing away the skin, all the way up through her abdomen. The hulk was now able to push even deeper, and blood squirted and splashed against its translucent ivory skin with every pound and thrust. The blood ran along the edges of the platform and collected in a wide glassy puddle on the floor.

The woman continued to scream, but as she did this, the creep would stuff its hand even deeper into her throat. Then she'd gag. Thick ropes of mucus dangled from her lips as she desperately tried to catch her breath. The brute relentlessly continued to fuck her wound.

The creeps dug their fingernails into her arms and legs, and spread her even farther apart, which came easier now that she was quite literally splitting apart. They bit and pinched her nipples, and slapped her breasts until they became so red and bruised that her pink tattooed moon was no longer visible. The brute leaned over and gripped the platform beneath her for leverage. It was then able to penetrate so deeply her body split all the way up through her breasts, until it was fucking nothing more than a puddle of loose organs.

At some point, her heart stopped beating. It had to have, though it was unclear when.

The hulk continued to fuck her, long after death, spilling her juices onto the platform and the ground below. By the time the beast finally reached orgasm, her body was split completely in two and its pearly white seed swirled and swam in the pool of viscera and blood, turning the gore puddle a warm pale pastel pink. Thick strings of it rolled off the platform and puddled along the floor. The hulk leaned in close to sniff the odorous stew of meat, blood, sex, and semen. Its cock seemed to swell and twitch as it did this. It sifted through the gore, trying to find whatever was left of her head. Again it dug its fat fingers into her mouth, pinched her tiny teeth between its fingers and broke each of them off, one by one, taking them as some sort of souvenir. *Trophies.*

Once it was finished, the smaller creeps feasted on what remained.

12.

And the nightmares continued.

This time I seemed to be dreaming with my eyes open, as I could see my bed, the sheets draped over me, and a window to my direct right. I knew, even in my dream, this was a lie. This was not where I was resting, or where I was struck unconscious. I was in some unfamiliar room. In reality, I was still out there, somewhere on the street in front of the diner, burning and melting in front of the crowd.

Even though I knew these things, I still couldn't force myself awake.

I continued to dream. A woman in a white nightgown stood on the other side of the window. She was wearing a white plastic mask over her face. She raised her left hand and held up three fingers.

I tried to move my arms, my legs, my mouth, but I was paralyzed and silent. Sleep paralysis. All I could do was watch her as she watched me.

The woman in the window lowered one of her fingers, now showing only two.

She then lowered another finger.

What was she doing? Counting down? Counting down to what?

She lowered the remaining finger, now holding up only a fist. With her other hand, she pulled the mask away from her face, revealing a large telephone receiver instead of what should have been a human head.

"Danger, Finn McKenna. Danger," a whispering voice said. The voice was calling to me from the telephone receiver.

Still unable to move, I turned my eyes away from the woman and looked down at my own body. My arms and legs were twitching, not unlike those of a dying insect's.

The phone was ringing.
The phone was ringing.
The phone was ringing.

13.

The phone continued to ring, echoing out for miles, but there was no one around to hear it. It was cold and it was dark, but not in the way a desert should be. There was a presence in Peligro. A ghost. A demon. A haunting. Something. Something was there, and it was not human.

The phone was ringing.
The phone was ringing.
The phone was ringing.

Tiny insect legs protruded from the ear and mouthpiece of the hand receiver until they stretched so far their tiny black bodies began to slop out of the holes.

Crickets, suddenly thousands of them.

More legs reached out from the receiver. Cricket bodies continued to pour out in bucket loads. The insects were screeching, singing, playing their godless symphonies for no one.

The phone was ringing.
The phone was ringing.
The phone was ringing.

14.

The nightmares seemed to loosen their grip, as I was finally able to open my eyes, without dreaming, at least it certainly didn't *feel* like a dream anymore. My eyes were open, but I could see nothing. The area around me was completely dark. Not even the faintest sign of light was visible. I pressed the heels of my palms against my eyes, trying to rub out the blindness, but it didn't help. For a moment, my heart began to flutter and I panicked at the thought of the blindness being a permanent effect of the coma, but I decided to rule out all other possibilities before accepting this to be truth. I swam inside the darkness, feeling around frantically for something to hold onto, something I would recognize through only touch, but there was nothing but the ground beneath my feet, or so it seemed.

Cold stones and dirty ground.

15.

I found a staircase hidden in the darkness. I crawled up on my hands and knees, staring blankly into the blackness before me, feeling the walls, the wood of the stairs, the air above me. I felt as if I were a ghost, a wisp of ectoplasm hanging in darkness. My fingertips were acting as my eyes. At the top of the staircase I came to a dead end. The stairs led straight into a cold stone wall. A stairway for ghosts. There was nothing.

As I turned to head back down the stairs, something caught my eye. A sliver of light, barely visible, but it was there. Above me. I was relieved to discover that I wasn't blind, just engulfed in darkness. I reached up towards the ceiling, pressed my shoulder against it and heaved. The wooden boards lifted, revealing a secret: it was not a ceiling at all, but rather a hidden door. I swung the door open and it crashed against the floor on the other side. A handful of dust took flight and sparkled in the daylight slipping in through the windows.

I was in an unknown house. An abandoned, run down, broken, empty house. I wasn't sure how I'd gotten there, or more worryingly *who* it was that brought me there. I wondered about the condition of my body, if I had melted any more than before. I looked at my fin hand. It certainly looked worse.

A disturbance sounded in the distance, in one of the rooms of the old house. Glass shattered. Someone else was in the house with me.

I slowly and carefully walked across the floor, trying to make as little noise as possible. I could hear what sounded to be the rambling of a drunken old man.

"Goddamn it, Tom," the voice mumbled, barely audible. "That was the last of it. That was it. Nice going, hot shot."

I followed the voice to an open room and down a short hallway. I stood at the end of it, back against the wall, trying to get a good look at the source of the voice. I peeked over the edge of the wall. In the kitchen area there was an older man, probably in his mid-sixties, sweeping up glass from the kitchen floor. The glass was wet with what smelled like cheap whiskey. He appeared to be talking to himself.

"Tom, Tom, Tom," he said, pulling a cigarette out of his sport coat pocket and lighting up. "How'd you ever make it this far, Tom?" He paused and took a long drag from his cigarette. Exhaled. "Luck. That's all it is, old man. Luck."

He ashed on the floor, which caused the spilled whiskey to catch fire. His eyes widened and immediately he stomped the small blaze out with his boots, despite the slowness and carelessness of his stomps.

I shifted my weight from my right foot to my left, causing the floorboards in the hallway to creak under the pressure. In an instant, a butcher's knife hurled through the air and buried itself into the wall right next to my head, only an inch away from my ear.

16.

"Oh sorry... *shit*," the man in the kitchen said. "I wasn't thinking. Thought you were one of *them*." He continued stomping out the fire, which by then had attached itself to the bottoms of his pant legs.

I reached up, pulled the knife out of the wall, and walked over to the old man.

"I'll get water," I said, walking to the kitchen sink.

"It's no use," the old man said. "The tap is dry. This place hasn't had running water since…hell, ever, for all I know."

I twisted the knobs of the faucet. Nothing came out.

"You always were a goddamn hardheaded punk," the old man muttered, finally managing to extinguish the last of the flames with his boots.

"Excuse me?"

"I just told you there wasn't any water, and you checked anyway. You think I'd lie to you?"

"No," Finn said, shaking his head.

The old man wiped the sweat from his forehead with the end of his shirt. "It's because I'm old then? Senile, you think?"

I didn't know how to respond.

"Ha! I'm only joshing you, Finny," the old man said, laughing. "You think you'd know me better after all these years…"

I furrowed my brow in confusion.

"Know you? Have we met?"

The old man cocked his head inquisitively, squinting his eyes into tiny coin slots. He walked towards me and took another draw from his cigarette. With his free hand he spread apart the eyelids of my left eye, studying with deep concentration.

"You serious?" the old man asked, smoke leaking out from between his teeth. "You really don't remember me?"

My heart beat so rapidly I could actually feel it swelling through the bones of my ribcage.

"No. I honestly don't remember… *anything*."

17.

Smoke clouded the kitchen and drifted through the house. The smell of burning wood overpowered all other smells. The old man cupped his hands over his mouth and blew hot breath into his hands. He unfolded them and placed them over my face.

"I need you to relax," the old man said. I nodded. "Do you know your name?"

"McKenna. Finn McKenna."

"Do you know the date?"

I thought for a moment.

"No."

"Do you know what state you're in?"

"Texas."

"Do you know of the war?"

"No."

The old man took a short puff from his cigarette and again placed his hands over my face.

"Do you know of Demolition Ya Ya?"

"Yes…well, sort of."

"Do you know of Tom Stripper?"

"No."

"I'm Tom Stripper."

"Oh."

"Do you know of Polly Pinkerton?"

"Pinky?"

"Yes. So, you remember her?"

"I called her from a payphone hours ago. Her number was written on my arm. I think she's in trouble."

"You *called* her? Why the hell would you do that? The game isn't over yet."

"I didn't know."

The man wiped sweat away from his brow with the back of his hand and pushed the cigarette to his lips.

"She's more than in trouble, kid. How long ago was it you say you called?"

"A few hours...well, I think. I'm not sure. How long have I been here with you?"

The man looked away, ran his fingers through his hair, and sighed.

"Polly Pinkerton is dead, kid."

18.

"I had a dream about her," I muttered under my breath.

"About who?" asked Tom.

"About Pinky. At least I think it was her."

Tom pulled out another cigarette from his shirt pocket and lit it with the butt of one already in his mouth. "Dreams are shit kid. They don't mean nothin'."

"But still… it was terrifying. There was this crowd of brutes, they were holding her down…pinning her to the ground…one of them raped her."

Tom scratched at the scruff under his chin in a nervous manner.

"These brutes…were they *Ya Ya* brutes?"

"I don't know. They were strange white…hulks…beasts. *Monsters.* By the end they were all covered in blood…her blood. Pinky's blood. They ripped her apart."

"Monsters?"

"Monsters. Fucking heartless bastards," I said.

I stared off into the distance, lost in the visions of the nightmare looping continuously in my brain. Tom saw the pain in my eyes, I could tell by his silence.

"It may be some distorted memory. Maybe it wasn't her," he said.

"She had a pink moon tattooed on one of her breasts," I said.

Tom closed his eyes and squeezed the arch of his nose.

"A moon, you say?" he asked.

"Yes."

He paused. Something clearly weighed heavily on his mind.

"Like I said, kid…dreams are shit. They don't mean a goddamn thing."

I shook my head and studied my deformed hands.

"I'm scared, Tom. I'm melting."

Tom looked over at me and took another puff.

"I know, kid. I know."

19.

In the morning, Tom stuffed a small sack full of supplies—a candle, matches, a pair of scissors, and anything else he could find laying around the house that would maybe come of use later on. I'd fallen asleep on the hard wood floor, using a dusty old curtain as a blanket. Tom lit his morning cigarette, and the smoke swirled like dust in the sunlight.

"Kid," Tom said. His voice tore wickedly through the silence. "We have to get a move on. If we leave now, we can make it to our brute by sundown."

My bloodshot eyes opened and flickered like television static.

"Brute? What do you mean *our brute?*" I asked.

"You're still playing the game, aren't you?"

"Demolition Ya Ya?"

Tom nodded.

"You're still in, right?" he asked.

I sat up, tossing my dusty blanket aside.

"Yeah, I'm still in," I said.

"Then we need to go."

20.

We walked the scorched road.

"I've worried about you, you know?" Tom said.

"Why is that?" I asked.

"They hit you pretty hard on that first attack. I thought I was seeing the end of the great Finn McKenna. It's a scary thing to witness."

"I was attacked?"

"*We* were attacked. Sorry, I keep forgetting you're brain-fucked." Tom lit another cigarette. He smoked as if it fueled his voice. "So, there we were, in the middle of the desert. We were in Jaxx—oh, ah, Bonejaxx—our brute."

"Wait, I keep hearing this word: *brute*. What is it exactly? A vehicle?"

"Well, yeah, I guess you could call it a vehicle. It's the machine we use to compete in Demolition Ya Ya. It's basically a giant fighting robot. All the runners are assigned to one."

"Runners?"

"Runners, you know…us, the contestants, I guess you could say."

"So, we're the *runners?* And you and I, we have a giant machine called *Bonejaxx?*"

Tom exhaled and his nostrils flared and smoked like a burning building.

"That's the gist of it, yes," he said.

"Sorry. Okay, so we were attacked?"

"Well, we crossed paths with another set of runners who were driving a brute called *RazorPriest*. Their brute's attack was simple, but effective. It had a hydraulic hammer attached to its top that would swing down and pin us to the dirt, all the while a long steel spear would shoot out of its side—in and out, in and out, in and out—and stab at us. It messed Jaxx up pretty damn bad and it threw you clear from your station, which is actually a good thing, cause the Priest thought we were stone cold dead after that and took off, prowling for its next victim. I know it fucked you up in a bad way, but it's *pure luck* you were thrown out, else we may not have made it through alive."

"I don't understand. What does me being thrown out have anything to do with us surviving the attack?"

"Haven't you figured it out yet, Finny? *The lightning, the electric touch, the melting skin?*"

"I don't know what you mean," I said.

Tom flipped the spent butt of his cigarette out into the distance.

"You're the battery."

21.

"You see, all us runners are here for a reason. We all possess tiny gifts. You're an engineer. You build things. You were the one that came up with the design of your bones."

I rubbed the edge of my palm along my ribcage.

"My bones?"

"Your bones are not *bones*. Not anymore," Tom dug into his pocket, retrieving his pack of cigarettes. The pack was empty. He tossed it to the sand and dug out a brand new one.

"You smoke a lot," I said.

Tom nodded his head.

"Yeah, I know, kid. You probably won't believe me, but I'm getting better, cutting back. I used to hold a cigarette between every finger, smoke four at a time."

"Are you serious?"

Tom pushed a fresh cigarette to his lips and toked up.

"Shut the hell up, kid, and pay attention. I was telling you about your bones. This is important."

22.

"You replaced your *bone bones* with *lead bones*. Your lead bones have some sort of alkaline electrolyte marrow, same stuff found in reusable batteries. The lightning that keeps kicking your ass was your idea, too. That's how you recharge."

"But how does the lightning find me? It seems like every time I walk twenty feet I get hit by it."

"Come on, Finny, my boy, you're smarter than this. I know your memory is gone, but hell, you should have figured this all out by now."

"I don't know, Tom. I'm trying."

"Lightning rods, kid…you've got lightning rods coiled around your bones and whenever you get hit, you're recharged."

"And that's why I'm melting?"

"That's why you're melting."

I looked down at my fin hand. The ridges of my fingers were nearly non-existent. No one would have ever guessed it once was a fully functional fist, complete with individual moving digits. I did my best to keep the fingers on my other hand separated, but I could already feel them getting sticky. It was only a matter of time.

"So what about you? Do you have any kind of secret powers? What's your purpose here?"

"What's my purpose here? Hmmm," he squinted his eyes and inhaled a lungful of smoke. He held it in this time. "I guess you could say I'm pretty good at fixing things."

23.

The sun was setting again, appearing to choke the life from the sky in the way it turned pink, red, dark blue, then finally black. Death was darkness and darkness was death. No good would come of the night. I worried about dreaming, about seeing her and feeling hopeless again. The visions couldn't repeat themselves another night. I wouldn't be able to take it. I tried pushing the thought deep into the recesses of my mind and continued marching through the desert, thinking instead of the game and my place within it.

Just before dusk, we arrived at our destination: *Bonejaxx*. Right where we left it, half buried in the steaming sands of the desert.

"Well, here we are," Tom said. "I suggest we set up camp. We'll head out in the morning."

I looked up at Bonejaxx, a mammoth of electric metal, and tossed my pack to the sand. As much as I feared dreaming, I couldn't stand to stay awake much longer. My body was weak and in desperate need of rest.

"Night," I said.

"Night."

24.

"Tom?" My voice sliced through the darkness and startled Tom awake.

"Shit, kid…you scared the living daylights out of me. I was dreaming."

"Sorry, I just have one more question."

"Shoot," he said.

"Can you tell me about Polly Pinkerton?"

He let out a depressed sigh.

"In the morning, if you still want to know, I'll tell you. But trust me, kid, you don't want to know. Get some sleep."

25.

The floor of the desert seemed to be disappearing. What appeared to be a black hole, or some portal, some direct connection between Peligro, TX and Hell itself, was slowly expanding and consuming all in its path. Except looks can be deceiving. Sometimes things aren't exactly as they appear to be. Sometimes it takes a closer inspection to really get an idea of what things are and how they got that way. This black hole, for example, upon closer inspection was actually an orgy of insects consuming the earth. It's funny the things we see when we're paying attention...

The source of the swarm was inside the lone phone booth. The mouthpiece of the telephone receiver came loose and crickets continued to spill out like a living, twitching waterfall. The crickets screeched and howled at the moon. The Devil's symphony.

The insects swallowed the desert, swallowed the stale night air, and swallowed the darkness—a devastation swarm.

Perhaps it still could've been called a black hole, as it seemed to be just as destructive, though I supposed by definition I would have been incorrect labeling it as such. Somehow this seemed worse.

26.

There were no other dreams that night, just crickets. If the dream was true, then the waitress at the diner was right, the crickets sure were bad this year. I'd never seen anything quite like it. Of course, at the time I hadn't put much thought into those dreams, as they seemed so insignificant when compared to the others I was having then, of Polly, of Pinky, whatever her name was.

When morning came, I held off on asking about her again. I wasn't entirely sure I wanted to know anymore. Tom seemed to think the information would damage me in some way, and I certainly didn't need any more of that. I looked down at my fin hand and could see the bone of my index finger piercing out of the gummy flesh. The pain should have been excruciating, but it wasn't in the slightest. I felt nothing but the tingling sensation of numbness.

Tom woke about twenty minutes after I did. He wiped the dust from his face and coughed for what seemed like days. He patted his pockets for his cigarettes, pulled out one from the pack and pushed the filter to his lips.

"Morning," he said, then lit up.

I nodded at him and took a final breath of fresh air before the smoke leaking out from his nostrils tainted it. He looked up at the defeated machine before us.

"You think you can fix it?" I asked.

He laughed.

"What do you think I've been doing all this time, kid?" he said. "While you've been out sleeping here and there, staggering around like some helpless fool, getting bullied by thugs, melting, falling into comas, you name it, I've been right here fixing this goddamn thing. All it needs now is the battery."

He points at me.

"You, kid," he said. "You're up."

The muscles in my arms and legs tensed. I was nervous I'd become too weak to fuel the machine.

"Half my body is numb," I said. "I don't think I can do this."

"Perfect. The numbness means you're charged," he said. "That last storm did you good. When I saw the lightning dart out of the sky, all bolts headed in the same direction, I knew exactly where to find you."

I tried balling my fin hand into a fist, but only managed to get halfway there. I wasn't in total control of my body, that much was certain, and I wasn't ready for whatever it was I was about to do. I looked up at the machine. It was toppled over and half-buried in the sand. I felt fear creep into my soul.

"This is me," Tom said, pointing at the carriage in the front. "You're in back."

27.

The machine sort of looked like a giant insect, dead in the sand. It had six appendages: two legs and four arms, and a head that jutted out from the middle of its torso, with red eyes and an exposed, wired electric brain. Its exoskeleton was made of some sort of metal, but looked more like bone from a distance. Each of its power-driven hands held a gun. Two with fully-automatic rifles and the other two gripped a larger gun, something completely unconventional, one that resembled the underbelly of a hornet, except with a sting a thousand times worse than that of any insect.

    I crawled up onto the rear, which was nothing more than a narrow slot, just wide enough for my body to slip inside. The space inside BoneJaxx was cramped, but not completely uncomfortable. My arms naturally slipped inside two cylindrical chambers in front of me, as if I somehow saw through the fog that was my memory and remembered exactly what it was I was supposed to do. I couldn't deny the intelligence of the involuntary actions of my arms. They certainly knew where to be, what to do, and how to do it. Because of this, for the first time since waking in the desert, I started to feel hope that my memory would eventually return, and that it had perhaps started to already. I was feeling electric, and not just with an overwhelming feeling of hopefulness and joy, but *truly electric*. Surely it had something to do with the metal poles now gripped in my soft palms (located at the end of the chambers I'd slipped my arms into), because at first contact I instantly felt a rush of blood pulsing through me, or perhaps it was adrenaline. Whatever it was, I felt fantastic.

There was a hollowed-out area in the chamber, just at eye level, that contained a thickly padded oval pillow. Clearly the space was designed for a face to be pressed against it, so that's exactly what I did. Immediately, I felt as if I had become a part of the machine myself. Once I placed my face into the brute's core, I was greeted with an electric vision of the landscape surrounding the machine. I had direct access to its eyes, the two red-lensed cameras poking outward through the deep sockets of its metal skull, and the sight brought on a surreal feeling within me, as if I had actually become the living, breathing BoneJaxx. There was an undeniable connection between me and the machine. We were one. Somehow just through touch alone, my nervous system had interlaced with the inner workings of the machine and *I was in control.* I could make it move in any manner I desired through thought alone. *I actually remembered this!* It was as if the machine had rebooted my brain and my thoughts and memories all came rushing into me all in an instant (although it felt that way in the moment, unfortunately I'd soon discover large gaps of information were still unaccounted for). Using my newfound knowledge, I pulled the brute up onto its feet and as I did this, a faint humming sound buzzed in my ears, followed by the crackling of static.

"That's it, kid! I knew you were ready," Tom's voice spoke to me through an internal speaker mounted on the surface area located next to my left ear.

"This feels incredible," I said, feeling the electricity moving through me.

"Well don't get your jollies off just yet, we have work to do," he said. "Check out the radar. RazorPriest is just outside the city."

I looked at the radar displayed in the top right corner of my electric vision. There was a single red dot pulsating, giving the precise location of the brute. According to radar, RazorPriest was just a few miles away.

"Looks like we're all that's left, kid," Tom said. "No other blips on radar. If we take it down, we'll win Demolition Ya Ya."

Whatever was about to happen, I now felt more than ready for it. The electricity brought on an overwhelming amount of energy that I could not wait to expel.

"So we just go to it then, huh?" I asked, still feeling a little clouded.

"Nah, we've got a better way," he said. "Check this out."

The robot lifted its arms so that all four were stretched out in front of us, then what looked to be a cloth sail dropped out of each limb, catching what little breeze was present and instantly expanding in glorious breaths. Each pair of arms crossed over one another, and the serrated edges of the left rubbed against the smooth edges of the right, creating a haunting symphony of sound. The vibrations moved along the sails, which helped project the sound out into the distance.

"What is this, Tom? What are we doing?" I asked.

"Making it come to us," he said. "Neat little trick, huh? Learned this one from the crickets. They're bad this year. Can't avoid 'em."

"How will it know to find us? Don't they think they've already taken us out of the game?"

"Yeah, they think they've won. Probably why they're so close to the city. Looks like they were headed back to claim their victory," he said, then chuckled. "Probably already started celebrating, the bastards. Once they hear this, they'll check their radars and see we're still very much in the game. Won't take 'em long to get here, just you watch. Man, I wish we could see their faces right now."

"You think they'll hear it? They're pretty far away," I asked.

"Oh, they'll hear it. Don't you worry."

28.

"I know it's last minute, but let's go over controls and strategy," Tom said.

A rush of panic shuddered through me.

"Okay," I said, with a nervous quiver in my voice.

"You control about ninety percent of this thing. You tell it where to move, where to step, jump, roll, all that. You also control the outer pair of arms, the ones with the assault rifles attached. Got it?"

"Got it," I said.

"I'll keep an eye on the gauges and work the inner arms, the bug gun."

"Okay, so we're clear on controls. What about strategy?"

"Do you believe in god?"

I thought about it for a second.

"I don't know," I said, disappointed I hadn't remembered as much as I had hoped.

"Well, if you find god in the next few minutes, praying is an option. There ain't much we can do but fight like all hell against that thing."

"That's all you've got?"

"That's all I've got," he said. "Oh, well, I guess just look out for that hammer swinging overhead. Don't let it pin us to the ground like last time. And avoid the impaler. And the razors."

"Tom, seriously?"

He laughed.

"I hate to say it, kid, but I am as serious as a heart attack."

A lump formed in my throat. We'd be dead in minutes. This was it. My existence, as far as I knew, had only consisted of the events that happened between waking in the desert and what was happening now. All the confusion, emotions, the nightmares (*or were they memories?*) were all I was and would ever be. *Hell of a life.*

In the distance came the unmistakable sounds of a brute marching, and quite fast, if you ask me. It wasn't long before it was finally in our sights. There before us, in all its glory, was the RazorPriest. It appeared to be in rough condition, due to all the fights it had been in throughout the game, but it was still operational. By the looks of it, the runners inside the Priest were pissed as all hell to learn Tom and I survived the previous attack. Their machine stood a hair taller than ours, and was easily twice as broad. It certainly looked more modern than ours, as it had a sleek red finish and a collage of spherical shapes worked into its design, making it seem like the thing was sent back through time to destroy us. It had no limbs. Instead, it moved across the desert via a hover device on its base. Where one would expect the arms to be located, there were only spheres with deep slots through the centers. Attached to its backside was the hammer Tom warned me about. It resembled a scorpion's tail in the way of its mechanics, resting behind at ease, but in a moments notice would whip over the brute's topside and pummel whatever stood in its path. The closer it moved toward us, the more nervous I became.

We were the first to strike.

As I stood motionless, my mind blank from the stress of seeing this nightmare play out in front of me, Tom fired the first shot from the bug gun. I was surprised to see the gun did not shoot in the typical way, bullets or lasers flying, but instead darted a harpoon that lodged itself into the neck of the Priest. A wire was attached at the end of the harpoon that trailed back into the barrel of the gun. Bursts of electrodes carried through the wire, unloading into the brute, causing the machine to hiccup and spasm. It was able to rip the harpoon from its neck though. It tossed the spear to the sand. Spinning razorblades, about three feet in diameter, rose through the slots in the spheres at each of its shoulders, and as it charged at us, the razors dug deep into the steel bones of BoneJaxx.

Tom fired another shot.

"You awake back there, kid?" Tom asked.

I shook off the daze.

"Yeah, sorry. Just froze up," I said.

"Well, anytime you want to join in, that'd be great," he said.

The Priest again removed the harpoon from its body without much difficulty. I pulled BoneJaxx to the side and shot a barrage of bullets all in the Priest's direction. Most of the hits landed, piercing the outer steel shell of its body, but they didn't seem to destroy any of the inner mechanics of the machine, as it wasn't phased in the slightest.

"Keep your eyes up, kid," Tom said, and just as he said it, the hammer behind RazorPriest swung overhead and caught our brute right in the middle of its back, just outside the cockpit area I was standing inside. The force of the hammer caused the entire backside to bend inward, pushing the edges of the steel wall directly into the flesh of my back. The pain wasn't immediate, but when it hit, I howled and struggled to get free from its grasp. I was pinned inside the brute, and the thought of being stuck inside the machine was enough to raise my state of panic to a whole new level.

"You okay?" Tom asked.

"No. I've been hit. I'm bleeding out," I said.

"Bleeding out? How bad is it? You gonna make it, kid?"

"I can't tell, but there's plenty of blood pouring out of me right now. I can feel it streaming down my legs," I said, trying to take comfort in feeling that no vital organs had been pierced, but it really wasn't helping to calm me any. As long as I could keep my panic under control, I could get through this. *Do not go into shock*, I told myself. *Things will be okay.* I couldn't convince myself it was true.

Not sparing a second, the Priest dug a razor through the torso of our brute and Tom immediately lifted the arms, placing the bug gun behind its head and pulling it close. It was pinned now against our chest, an intelligent move in theory, however, it proved to be a fatal mistake. The Priest swung the hammer overhead once again, hitting the same place it did before and pushing the metal even deeper into my flesh. *I was done.* I couldn't think anymore for all the pain, and as a result BoneJaxx fell limp. Its knees fell to the sand. Tom held his grip on the machine and it held its grip on us, holding the hammer against our back and steadily increasing the pressure. I felt close to losing consciousness, which is probably why I didn't feel a thing when the Preist struck us with the impaler. It pierced our body seven times.

Before fading into unconsciousness, I managed to utter a single word:

"Tom?"

Tom did not respond.

29.

Peligro…

    The cricket swarm covered the earth now, so much so that even the single lamppost in that empty desert was covered so thick with pests that it didn't appear to be putting off any light whatsoever. A sea of darkness within darkness.

    If one were to see, however, the unnerving vision of the earth opening deep within the swarm, it would have polluted their mind, causing them to feel as if they were slipping into some sort of madness in the way it all seemed too surreal, too nightmarish, to truly exist. Those all-seeing eyes would also be privy to the haunting vision of a body being pulled out of the ground, being pulled out by the crickets themselves, and unknowing too if the body was being pulled out from some grave or from some Hell that existed deep below the sands of the desert. What evil brings this, the mind belonging to those eyes would think, because it would know these sorts of things didn't happen in real life. It couldn't exist. Things like this simply did not happen.

    This was an impossibility.

    A glitch.

    But yet, there it was.

    And the eyes would see the body belonged to a woman, a beautiful young woman with ivory skin and long flowing hair, so blond it almost appeared white. The eyes would also see the body was without clothing, and that there was a tattoo around her right areola, a tattoo of a pink crescent moon.

  The insects carried the body deeper into the darkness, and those who didn't help, followed. And supposing those eyes were still gazing upon the sand and the scene that just played out before it, then they would also find that the light from the lamppost had returned, once again illuminating the busted up phone booth that stood on the sands next to it. And the ears belonging to those eyes would hear the ringing telephone just on the other side of the mangled doorway, causing the feet belonging to those eyes to step closer, and when they stood close enough to the booth, they could peek inside and see the telephone was vibrating violently in its cradle with every ring. And if they were to look even closer, they would see the handwritten sign posted on the rectangular frame of the phone, just below the coin slot, the sign that read:

  "TO REACH THIS PAYPHONE, DIAL 859-279-8094"

  The phone was ringing.
  The phone was ringing.
  The phone was ringing.

30.

When I awakened [truly, finally awakened?], Penelope was cradling my head in her arms. I couldn't see her doing this, of course, due to the blindness, but I could hear her chanting some god-loving Mexican gospel something or other as she rocked me back into consciousness. Guess the goddamn electric night caused me to collapse and suffocate again. Seemed like it was happening more and more with every passing squall. I must have been out cold longer than usual that time, cause she screamed with joy the moment she noticed I was awake. *Must have been one hell of a storm!* Goddamn if I couldn't remember it, though. My disgusting, fat-ass lump of a body must have been dancing all through the night! Oh, that sweet electric sky was all I lived for in those days.

  Penelope propped me up against the wall and proceeded to feed my maw with a handful of pills. I couldn't refuse. Hell, I couldn't even spit the damn things out, I was such a weak animal. She pushed my head up, so my face was pointed toward the ceiling, then worked the muscles in my throat with her hands to make the pills go down. She continued to speak some happy-sounding

Spanish words and even playfully patted my cheeks. *That bitch. She was only happy cause her job was safe! She was worried she'd have to spend another year in the unemployment office, trying to get set up with some other unfortunate asshole who couldn't take care of himself, and hoping she'd get someone with more riches next time, more things to stuff inside her bags and claim as her own!* I knew her too well, that Penelope. She always was a clever thief.

Then, for the first time I'd ever experienced anyway, Penelope finally said something I actually understood:

"Mister Gordon! Mister Gordon! He is awake," she said. Her English was terrible, so of course it sounded garbled and mumbled and wrong.

All in an instant, I felt His presence in the room. I couldn't quite explain it, but even had I not heard Penelope call out his name, I would have realized exactly who it was at my door, *inside my home*! It was Gordon. *The* Gordon. For once in my life I was happy to be blind. The evil that man carried with Him, it was enough to send a chill through my soul just knowing He was near. I couldn't imagine having to look him in the eyes. I wish I could have spoken to Him though. *Oh, the things I would have said!*

"Bricker," he said to me. I hadn't heard my name uttered in so long, I almost forgot it belonged to me.

"We have to reset," he continued. "Pinky has gone off chart again."

Pinky. Polly Pinkerton. 1978. *Memories swirled...*

Gordon stepped closer to me, running his hand through the hair on the backside of my head.

"I know you don't remember, but we've reset before," he said. "It's nothing to worry about. You'll feel a slight pinch, then nothing at all. Next thing you know, you'll be safe at the beginning again."

He was right. I didn't remember. I hadn't the slightest idea what he was talking about.

"Oh, just so you know, the tests are coming along great. You've really proved yourself to be the lifeblood of this experiment. You're the *battery* that keeps this thing running. You should see my notes! I'll share them with you soon, maybe after two or three more rounds. How does that sound?"

I couldn't respond. I wasn't even sure I would had I been able.

"Alright, so here we go," he said, and then I felt the slight pinch he was referring to.

It felt as if a needle had pierced clear through my brain, but the pain quickly faded.

"The reset for Channel Fourteen starts in three, two, —"

And after a sharp quick sting of electricity, my mind was suddenly somebody else's again...

[32] If You Don't Sleep, You Don't Dream.

XI

A beautiful woman enters the room.
It's the same woman I've been watching for the past week.
The same woman I fell in love with through the window.

This woman is my *daughter.*

She stands in the doorway, silently asking my permission to enter.

>   I'm sorry.

She puts her hand to her mouth.
The sound of my dreadful voice terrifies her.

>   I thought he was... hurting you.

Her eyes are pink and full of tears.
She walks into the room and takes a seat at
my bedside, reaching into her purse for a
tissue.

>   *I'm sorry about this.*
>   *I promised myself I wouldn't cry,*
>   *that I was strong enough to do this…to see you.*

She dabs the tissue against her eyes.

>   *Do you remember me?*

She holds her breath.
I don't remember her.
My own daughter, for the life of me I can't
remember being her father.

> No. I'm so sorry.

She closes her eyes and exhales.

> *The doctors told me you wouldn't,*
> *but I was certain...*

Her tears now a steady stream.

> *I mean, after all these years, you've found me.*
> *How can you not remember me?*

I don't know how to answer her question.
I avert my eye.
She reaches for another tissue.

> How did you know me?
> Back at your house, I mean.
> How did you know... I was your father?
> Surely you didn't recognize me, the hideous
> beast I've become.

> *It was your tattoo.*

I look down at my wrist.

There is a small black tattoo of a cricket.
Joan pulls back the cloth of her blouse that lay at her wrist, revealing a tattoo that matches mine exactly.

> *You got your tattoo after Seth—well...*

She chokes up again.

> *It's a memorial.*
> *Seth loved insects.*
> *He was always so strange.*
> *Like you, I guess.*

Joan laughs.
Her eyes are red and welling.

> *I got my tattoo much later,*
> *as a way of remembering you both.*

She stares at her wrist a moment.

> *You know, he looked just like you.*
> *Mom says that every time Seth comes up in conversation.*
> *She always said how proud you were of him.*

*Ah, mom... you know, I told her
about you finding me.
I guess she's really upset.
She hasn't spoken to me since.
But, you know, that's just how she is.
I think it would really do her good to see you.
Hopefully, she'll come around.*

Joan smiles brightly and walks toward the bed.

I'm just so happy to see you, Dad.

She wraps her arms around me and weeps again.
I return the gesture, but without feeling, just as anyone would holding a complete stranger in their arms.

XII

And then there it was, like a goddamn white rabbit pulled from my skull: Jellit Osborne!
Two minutes ago, I wouldn't have even recognized his name, but now my mind is plagued with it.

Jellit Osborne was a stain.

A hideous beast of a man, full of rage and fear.
Jellit Osborne was *another me.*
But he ran from Gordon…

Ten years ago, Osborne was on the front page of every major newspaper in this God-forsaken land, spreading stories about Gordon like a fucking pandemic.
The blood…
The scars…
The machine parts… complete with pictures labeled *'not for the squeamish.'*
His scars frightened, they did, though hardly comparable to the horrid seams that now hold my broken body together.

Everybody and their brother went looking for Gordon.
They were determined to run Him out of the hole He was hiding in.
To burn Him at the stake, they wanted!
Or maybe hack Him to pieces with an axe to match the grotesque body of the man they had all come to pity.

But they never found Gordon.

And after the sudden disappearance of Osborne, it didn't take long for the public to withdraw their fear and deposit it into the next major headline.
Detective Gray may be the only hunter left in the chase.

As for Jellit Osborne, Gordon silenced him in the most awful of ways.

Gordon always gets what he wants.

My pulse beats wildly.

XIII

A shiver breathes throughout every nerve.
I've been gagged, bound, bagged
...and drugged, though I suspect it's beginning to wear off.
Someone is dragging me by the collar through an impossibly rocky terrain.
Stones tear my skin.
I try to yell, but it only comes out as a moan.
The drugs.

We stop moving.

I'm released and my head falls to the ground, violently colliding with the sharp edge of a rock.
Then I'm blinded by a bright light as the cloth bag draped over my head is quickly removed.
Strange, the light is, when used to seeing only darkness.
A figure stands before the me, before the light.
A silhouette towers over me.
A cold steel blade slides along my cheek.
The gag is cut and removed from my mouth.

What have they done to you, Laz?

Asks a stern, booming voice.
Gordon's voice.

I want a comprehensive report.

Gordon?

I want a comprehensive report, Lazarus!

He says with great impatience.

Gordon...

I couldn't tell if it was the drugs, sheer happiness, or complete shock that kept me from saying anything other than His name.

Without warning, He digs His fingers into the not-quite-healed scar that runs along the width of my forehead.
The pain is surprisingly tolerable thanks to whatever chemical is flowing through my veins.
Blood drips from His fingers, onto my cheeks, and slides down my chin.
He's looking for the 'spider implant' that was removed weeks ago.
Gordon withdraws his fingers and grabs hold of my chin with alarming force.

What do you know, Lazarus?

My name is... Adam.

CHRIST!

Gordon leaps to His feet in a rage I've never seen before.
His silhouette grows as He moves closer to the light.

Then He swings His fist, takes hold of the light [a flashlight, I can see it now] and throws it against a nearby tree.
The flashlight blows apart, leaving us standing under only moonlight.
I can see now that we're in a field and that there are two other figures standing beside Gordon.
I feel a tightness in my chest when I see them. One of them is carrying a briefcase.

Gordon paces in an attempt to calm Himself. It seems to be working.

After a minute or two, He approaches me, His anger reserved.

What else did they tell you, my boy?

I hesitate, terrified to respond.
And at the same time I'm terrified *not* to respond.

They told me...

Yes?

They told me... you used me.

Gordon furrows His brow.

> *Used you? How?*

His madness returns.
I can see it in His eyes.

> *To commit crimes... to rape... for your pleasure... for your amusement...*

Gordon slugs my jawbone with remarkable force.

> *For my amusement?*
> *Lazarus, those women were essential sacrifices.*
> *The plan called for it!*

> Plan? What plan... Gordon?

> *You fool! You know nothing!*
> *What have we been doing these last twenty-eight years?*

The shock of not knowing who or what I am leaves me unable to speak.

> *Those doctors must have botched an operation or two, Lazarus.*

You should have remembered this!

Gordon walks toward to the two figures standing in the distance.
One of them reaches inside the briefcase and pulls out a small box, handing it to Gordon.
Gordon tosses it to me.

After this...

He opens the box in my hands.

...you will remember everything.

From the box, He removes a brick of confused cables,
a spaghetti-mess of wires, the size of a fist, and holds it prominently in his hand.

When you're ready, you'll know where to find me. I'll be waiting.

Gordon shoves the wire brick into my mouth and forces me to bite down on it.
Electricity surges throughout my body, sending waves of paralysis into every exhausted muscle.

I see a darkness, then I see it all.

XIV

Memories swirl...
There's a raging sea in the distance.
I watch as the waves leap and crash into one another.
Standing on the shore, the waters rush towards me and I stand with arms outstretched.
I welcome it.
I take a breath just before the dark water swallows me whole.

But something stops it, pushes it away.
A woman.
She touches me softly and wraps her arms around me, pushing her body against my back.
A familiar voice speaks to me.

>*Oh Adam, have you ever seen them so happy?*

To my left, two children...
my two children, Seth and Joan,
are smiling, laughing,
playing in the sand.

My wife, Mary, and I ... *are happy.*
My two children... *are happy.*
But somehow... they... *got away...*

Two hours later the police found Joan at a restaurant about 50 miles from the beach. Blood covered the lower half of her face and neck and there was a dark purple imprint on her forearm, the shape of a hand.
She told authorities a man had taken them, but couldn't offer a description.
She was in shock.
It's a wonder she was able to speak at all.
She said she had to use her teeth to tear a chunk of flesh from of her abductor's arm to get away.
She said Seth wasn't so lucky...

Police found his severed head a week later. They never found his body.

The fifteen years that followed his death are still hidden in a fog of pills and alcohol.
One thought always remained, though, the thought that somewhere out in the world the man who killed my son is walking free.

I became disgusted and suspicious of all men, and it only got worse with every passing year.
I became a recluse, ignoring the world, including my family, trusting only the pill, the bottle, and the gun.
All three led to my eventual arrest.

Walking alongside the highway [I was headed to buy more whiskey and no longer owned a vehicle] and a wicked thought came across my mind.
I couldn't quite explain it, why this thought popped into my mind at this particular moment, after all, I have never been a wicked man by nature.
Still, that didn't keep me from wondering... or acting on impulse.
I wondered what it felt like to just be driving by and see a man, such as myself, standing on the side of the highway, just as I was, aiming a gun straight at my face...
at my children... husbands... wives... loved ones.
Surely the taste of death would linger in the back of your throat, if even for an instant.
It must be exhilarating in a way, to think of how lucky it was you and your family got away, able to live life when all in one second you thought it was over.

You'd appreciate life more, the things you have and the people you share it with.
It could be a good thing, I must have told myself that.
Maybe I thought I wasn't being wicked.
Whatever the case, I withdrew my gun from the waistband of my jeans.
The power of God pulsed through my veins as the vehicles screeched and swerved across the road, that much I remember.
For that brief moment, I had the world at my mercy.
For the first time since my son's death, I felt in control.
And it felt good to be in control.

Not long after my arrest, I was visited by a man.
He only went by one name... Gordon.
He said He read an article about me in the newspaper.
About my son.
About his murder.
He could sense my complete discontent with the world.

He told me justice would soon be served, that the blood of those who sinned will soon flood the streets.

He asked me to join His army, promising me eternal life.
Eternal life!
He said He would come for me that very night, to break me out of prison.
I won't lie, I said sure and shook His hand, but secretly took Him for a fool and thought nothing more of His visit.

That night seven prison guards and several prisoners were killed in a violent explosion.
He came for me, just as He had promised.
After that, I believed every word.

The surgeries began soon after.

I was Gordon's first subject.
He was creating miracles!

He started with the women.
He collected them at night, one at a time, and injected a fertility drug into their bloodstream every morning.
Once he had enough, He would lay the women in rows across the bunker, naked, with their legs fastened taut in stirrups.
He would have me empty *my seed* into each of the women.

No matter how long it took, He always waited patiently.
Gordon said it had to be *my* seed, because I had a gift, and that gift needed to be shared with the world.

He said by doing this, we were speeding the process of evolution by what could have amounted to millions of years worth of *chance*.
I just did as I was told.

The fertility drug was necessary, not only for easy conception, but also because the women were having up to six children in one gestation, all born with my DNA.
Again, speeding the process of evolution.
I didn't know it at first, but Gordon was manufacturing an army.
This army would be raised by Gordon, from birth, allowing them to know nothing of the outside world.
These beings were superior to humankind, even as babies.
They were all gifted with an immortal gene, just like their father.

Of course, there were mistakes, those born without the immortal gene.
Those children were discarded.

Gordon stabbed every child in the heart when they were born, and those that didn't survive were ground into chow for the others.
This wasn't because Gordon was cruel, or because He was feeding some sick inner desire, it was out of *necessity*.
The children would not be cared for, so they were disposed of.
It was more humane than keeping them alive, believe me.

Gordon and His immortal army resided in a bunker below the city, until Gordon had built His army so large He had to build a new one.

Hell.
It was the only place big enough for us.
Hell was just outside the city, beneath a place called Steen Boneyard, a graveyard for unclaimed or unknown bodies.
The entrance was hidden, accessed only through the mouth of Poseidon, a stone fountain located in the center of the yard.

This is where Gordon is now, where he wants me to follow.
It's the only place I belong.

But before I go...

XV

I am standing at her door,
Mary's door, afraid to knock.
I've been standing here for an hour now.
I have so much to say.
I have nothing to say.
The hour of silence has built up inside of me,
I feel as if I could explode with emotions,
with words to speak to her,
my dear Mary,
but I fear I will never knock.
When I finally find the courage, I shout at the top of my seventy-eight year old lungs.

                                            I remember!

Startled birds scatter to the sky from the treetops.

                                    Mary! I remember!

There is terror in my voice... fear, shame, embarrassment.
I begin to weep.

                                   I remember, Mary!

> I remember...

My voice is consumed by emotion.
Time passes... seconds... maybe minutes...
Then a voice calls from behind the door.
She speaks to me.

> *Adam?*

I push my ear to the door.

> Mary?

> *Adam, what are you doing here?*

> I remember, Mary!
> I remember everything!

> *Do you remember how long it's been?*
> *Do you remember leaving me here to raise our daughter alone?*

> Yes. I know... I am sorry, Mary.

> *You have some nerve showing up here, Adam!*

Her voice has aged so much I don't even recognize it.

*You know, I visited you in the hospital
when Joan first told me you showed up at her house.
You were asleep.
I had every intention of going up there to confront you,
to let you know how much you've hurt me...
how you've hurt Joan...
but your scars...
it looks like you've already gotten what you deserve.*

I keep quiet.
She's still in so much pain.
The best I can do is to listen.

*You know, all this time I hoped
you committed suicide.
I mean, what kind of person does the
things you've done?
Abandoning your family.
Pulling a gun on innocent people.
You're sick.
He was my son too, Adam, and I didn't allow the
Devil inside me
like you did.
There's no excuse for the things you've done.*

She's right, and she doesn't even know the
half of my sins.
She loses control.
We're both weeping

on opposite sides of the door.

You know they found him...

She speaks soft and slow.
Regaining control.

Found who?

The man who murdered Seth.

What? When?

R A G E.

*Two years after you disappeared.
Brogan Spivey.*

Have you seen him?

*Only in the papers.
The only time I ever mustered up enough courage to
confront him,
I had a panic attack and went home before I even
got to the prison gates.*

We have to see him!
We have to go!

Come with me, Mary!

Adam...

Mary, we have to do this!
We *need* to do this!

When... now?

Yes, now!

Adam, you can't just expect me to leap
into your arms and go...
I can't do this... I haven't been able to do this...
in all these years, Adam...

Mary, I'll never forgive myself...
for what I did to you and to Joan.
You're right... I let the Devil in.
I don't deserve this... family.
But this is about... more than just us, Mary...
it's about
Seth... our little boy!
We deserve to have... our questions answered.
If you don't come with me today...
you'll never get that chance.
You won't allow yourself to.
I know, I've been gone...
for so long, but I am here... now...

and we'll be strong enough... together.

I'm staring at her door.
Her silence causes my hands to shake.

The door opens.

[5] The Edge That Would Not Speak

I felt the pain inside Adam's heart, the two of us sensing this lovely moment was quickly coming to a close, and possibly in the very worst of ways, so I decided to savor the moment and click away at the dial fastened to the side of my skull. I stopped on channel five, remembering the field and Rebecca and the goddamn electric moonlight. I couldn't help wondering if she ever broke free of her suffering, so I watched. It's all I could ever do...

The air thinned as the bullet train shot straight through the atmosphere, speeding away from Earth. I could see the curve of the planet now, for the first time ever, and the landmasses and oceans were growing smaller with every passing second. At the sight of it, I immediately became jealous, feeling as if I was the last living person to experience the view and the rush of emotions that came along with it. The ride was decades old now, and just about everyone I knew had been on it before. The Apollo Train, it was called. I remembered the commercials as if they had just announced the ride yesterday: *Come ride the Apollo Train. It's out of this world!* The idea of riding a train into space to visit the moon was almost unfathomable back in those days, but now, all these years later, it was just another forgotten thing.

Seeing my home planet from this distance overwhelmed me, which was surprising, as I had never really felt comfortable there, or anywhere for that matter. I had a disease, one that should have killed me at birth or shortly after, but didn't. At night I'd pray to anything that would listen, begging for something to take the breath from my lungs, to squeeze the life from my thundering heart, but every morning I'd awaken, full of pain and *life*. The only closeness I felt to the earth was the desire to be buried deep within it, so speeding on the train, catching a glimpse of the planet as it slid off into the distance shouldn't have been difficult to witness, yet it was, and my heart ached in a way I wished it hadn't, in love and in regret, instead of the way I hoped it would, a knife wound or massive heart attack.

Or cancer...why couldn't I have cancer? Life is always cured by cancer.

There was a buzzing coming from inside the pocket of my jeans. It was my cell phone. At first I was surprised to discover I had service all the way out in space, but after thinking of all those passengers over the years complaining of feeling disconnected from their virtual lives, it suddenly made a lot more sense. As depressing as it is to think about, it doesn't change the fact that it is absolutely true: if people are told they will experience something unique and incredible, but that in order to do so they must put down their phones and engage in real life, even if just for an evening, they will choose not to experience that unique and incredible thing, even if that thing is an evening in outer space *to have dinner on the fucking moon*, for fear of dealing with real life and engaging within a community without the safety net that is the world wide web. Come on, it's fucking space! Look out the window and take it all in! Contemplate life and the beauty of our own existence! *Ha, said the girl who came on this trip for no other reason than to die, and all with a buzzing cell phone in her pocket at that.* A walking contradiction, I was, am, and always will be. A priest not heeding the advice of her own cautionary sermons. A complete fucking mess.

Well, I most certainly was *different*. I hadn't trekked all those space miles for some lousy vacation, nor was I there to experience any taking in of the beauty of the scenery or for self-reflection or contemplation. I had a plan, always had. I'd thought hard about that exact moment, more than most people gave thought to anything. I wanted to die. *I needed to die.* And the moon was the only thing that could do that for me. *It owed me that.*

I looked down at my phone. It was a text from Kayla. She wanted to know if I'd made it to the moon yet. I told her *almost*, and thought it best to go ahead and mention its current phase [waning gibbous] because I knew it'd be the next question she'd ask. She wanted me to wave to her tonight. She said she'd be watching me from her bedroom window. I typed 'okay' and she responded with a smiley face emoticon. I buried the phone inside my pocket. I don't think Kayla ever believed I'd go through with it, with *my lunar suicide*. Possibly because I'd talk about it so damn much it just felt like normal to her now, but I was always serious. I didn't expect to come back from it. In all honesty, I didn't even expect to live long enough to wave to her happy ass down on earth that night either, but life would continue to shine its little light on me, despite my skull being reduced to an inch of dust—*but that part came later…*

The phone buzzed again. I let it be. There didn't seem to be a point in responding anymore anyway. I looked out the window and tried my damnedest to feel impressed knowing I was in outer space, but the truth was that it all just felt sort of hum-drum, probably because it looked exactly the way it did in every movie about an astronaut that ever existed. Watching movies equates to no surprises. It seemed I had experienced all there was to experience through watching movies. I'd felt every emotion, been through every kind of disaster, tragedy, and time period one could imagine, and all while wrapped in the fetal position, nestled on my couch. Looking out the window of the bullet train, the only feelings stirring within me were the ones associated with leaving home to kill myself, and even though those feelings didn't sit well in my gut, it still felt as if I'd made the right decision.

It was in that exact moment that I discovered the pain I normally felt every second of every day had been silenced, attributed likely to the adrenaline coursing then through my veins. It acted as some sort of venom, numbing me so I could slip silently and painlessly into death. The human body's interpretation of morphine. If I could somehow feel this way at all times, I wouldn't mind living forever. It felt ironic that the only way I could ever experience a life without pain was through the adrenaline rush of committing suicide. *Life*, man. *So fucking cruel.*

It didn't take long to get to the moon, as least not as long as I'd initially thought. The train slowed about a mile or two out and continued to slow until it came to a complete stop just outside the lunar station. An automated voice came over the intercom and my brain naturally tuned it out. Minutes passed and I was growing impatient that the doors still hadn't opened. It wasn't until I actually made an effort to listen to the automated voice that I discovered what the problem was.

"We have arrived at our destination, the moon. Please stand and remove the spacesuits from the overhead compartment. For your safety, the doors will not open until every passenger is fully suited."

Being the only passenger on the train, I stood and followed orders. I found it ridiculous dressing myself in a protective suit just so I could kill myself, but if that was the only way to get the doors open, I really had no other choice. Besides, after suiting up, the thought occurred to me that I should say something important before my death, even if there was no one around to hear it. I often fantasized about this moment, and now that it was here, *it should feel epic.* The words would have to be *perfect.* I'd think on it.

Just as I snapped the locks on my helmet to meet the metal ring running around the neckline of the suit, the doors gasped, releasing the pressurized oxygen from the cabin out into the moon's atmosphere, and slid open.

In my fantasies, at this moment I would leap from the ledge of the train, bounce in that airy, light gravity way all astronauts would do on television, then I'd release the locks of my helmet and spend my last dying breaths screaming at the moon's surface, cursing it, and burying my head into the dust as far as I could while sucking as much of it as possible into my lungs until they were filled to the throat with moon dust and my never-not-beating heart would finally stop and I would be no more. Disappointingly though, turns out that's not what happened at all. Instead, I was greeted by a small child.

He stood just outside the train. After stepping off the ledge, the young boy came no higher than my waist in height. He was towheaded and wore black swimming trunks and a grey t-shirt. His eyes were locked on mine as soon as the door released, as if he'd been staring into them long before the train ever arrived at the station. I didn't understand why he was there, but that wasn't what initially bothered me, it was *how* he was there, without a suit or protective gear of any sort. He was standing with his bare feet half covered in moon dust, breathing just as he would on earth, without any sort of apparatus.

Then he spoke.

"Where's Joan?" the boy asked, seemingly talking to *me*, even though I had never known a Joan in all my life.

I looked behind me, wondering if perhaps he was talking to someone else on the rock I had somehow not noticed. There was only the boy and me. I shook my head.

"I haven't seen her," I responded, immediately recognizing how odd a response it was. I felt as if I should have said more, perhaps I should have explained that I had never heard of such a person, or better yet, instead of even answering, I should have responded with a few questions of my own. *Who was this kid anyway? And what the fuck was he doing here on the moon?* Or the real head scratcher—*how the hell was he even alive?* But I didn't ask any of that. Instead, I waited patiently for him to speak again.

"Where's Joan?" he repeated.

That time I didn't respond. His eyes seemed to flicker as he spoke, as if they were two flames dying out.

"Where's Joan?" he asked. Blood trickled out of his nose and down along his lips and chin. He did not bother to clean himself. His stillness had me wondering if he'd even noticed the bleeding at all.

"Excuse me, do you know you're bleeding?" I asked.

The boy's eyebrows furrowed, as if he was having difficulty processing my words. It had me wondering if perhaps he was deaf. Then the thought occurred to me that we were in outer space. It felt silly forgetting a detail such as that, but the sudden appearance of the troubled boy, alone on the moon, had my brain scrambling for answers, some sort of explanation for his existence. It caused me to forget where I was and what I was supposed to be doing. Snapping back, I remembered something I'd once heard in my youth, something that stuck with me through the years: *sound does not travel in space, therefore it is impossible to speak and be heard*, at least that was my understanding of it. Still, even if that was the reason he could not hear me, it didn't explain why I was able to hear him. Perhaps there was some sort of scientific explanation for it, something about the composition of the moon's thin atmosphere or something of the sort, but I wouldn't know. All I really knew about the moon was that it owed me death, and I had come to collect that debt.

"Where's Joan?" he asked again, but before he'd even said her name this time half the boy's head caved in and blood sprayed violently from the wound, running down his cheek and the back of his head, and soaking into his t-shirt. Again, he seemed completely unaware any of this was happening.

The boy opened his mouth to speak again, most likely to repeat those same two words, but before he could do so, his body collapsed to the dusty surface of the moon. That's when I noticed the reason he fell, the skin and muscle that once covered the bones of his feet and calves had been gnawed off, and rather messily too. *By what? I wasn't sure.* There was nothing or no one around for miles as far as I could see. Curiously, the flesh around his knees and lower thighs vanished right before my eyes, with each little piece disappearing inch by inch, as if the child, right before me, was being eaten by some invisible pack of dogs. I thrusted my hands into the air around the boy's legs, trying to grab hold of whatever ethereal thing was behind all this, but could feel nothing.

I could not save him.

The boy wasn't left alone until every little strip of flesh had been torn clean off the bone. The curious creature left no evidence of its presence, no footprints or the like, only the bloody skeleton of the child, along with tiny bits of gore stuck between each bone, the parts of him not so easily accessible to invisible demon's wild maw. The stripped corpse rested in the dust before me and I could do nothing but stare at the nightmare. How strange, his eyes still seemed to watch me, even in death. It must have been only my imagination, but regardless, it still felt like the same fear to me.

Looking into his lifeless, lidless eyes is what led me to find the switch, a small button located on the center forehead of the boy's skull. I wasn't sure what it was at first glance, but upon closer inspection it most certainly was a switch, something installed in the child, an unnatural electrical attachment fused masterfully with his biology. Out of curiosity I pushed down on the switch and it moved deep into the skull until it clicked and held in place. Immediately the skeleton sprouted what looked to be iron wings, causing it to resemble some sort of mechanical angel drenched in bloody afterbirth. It rose from the dust and ascended into the heavens above.

    I wasn't sure what it was or what it wanted, but I hoped it was off to reunite with its beloved Joan. Restless spirits never make for warm company. I decided it best not to try and overanalyze the situation or else I would have driven myself mad trying to explain any small part of it logically. I took a step and bounced along the surface of the moon, making a new set of footprints in the dust. It had me wondering what it must have been like for those first few visitors, making tracks in dust that had been undisturbed for centuries. Walking there now it was almost impossible to distinguish my set of footprints from the thousands of others spread out in all directions and spanning the entire surface. The moon may have once been a surreal extraterrestrial landscape to the people of earth, but now it was just another vacation spot, and not even a popular one so much anymore. The allure quickly wore off once it became possible for everyday folk to travel there. The mysticism fell away like a pulled curtain the moment humans realized it was something they could *have*. It's always been human nature, after all, to want the things we know we cannot have and to dismiss them once we do.

Something strange happened then, and not surprisingly, if my trip so far was any indication of what was to come next: an airplane, a regular old jet airliner, came speeding through the black sky, hurdling straight towards the surface of the moon. It was coming down much too fast to make a clean landing. In retrospect, I probably should have high-tailed it out of there, somewhere away from the direct vicinity of the impact point and future debris field, but I didn't. I remained still and watched the diving airplane speed towards me the same way I would if it were only a 3D movie. The realization of the difference only came as it finally hit the surface. I could feel the impact and rumbling at my feet as the steel shell of the plane crumpled like a beer can, up in a crescent shape, until it resembled a furious scorpion with its tail prominently displayed overhead. The plane skittered continuously in my direction, tearing into the moon's terrain like jagged metal through skin, yet still I could do nothing but stare at its horrible beauty as it barreled toward me. I could not get my legs to run in either direction, to save my own life—as much as I tried, I could not think of a single reason to do so.

    The plane hit me, throwing my wilted body on top of it and snagging my spacesuit in the process. Material from the sleeve got pinched between two pieces of steel as the crash forged them together. I rode along, bouncing violently against the top of the plane as it pushed into the great sea of dust, until finally it came to an abrupt halt.

    To someone watching from a distance, not that anyone *was* (well, perhaps Kayla), I'm sure the wreckage was quite the sight. The plane didn't quite look like a plane anymore. It was bent in a C-shape, so that the ass-end of the thing was hanging over the cockpit, and split in several places, making the jagged metal resemble wicked tree limbs. Dust billowed and engulfed the plane, just as it would have on earth, despite the differences in gravity and atmospheric pressure. Flashes of light bathed the wreckage and the moon's surface as if there were storm clouds hanging overhead. The scene was quite surreal and dream- like, yet in that moment, I didn't question a thing. Perhaps it was due to my emotions and how caught up in death I was at the moment, blind to reality, like a young child receiving a love letter, but regardless of the answer, I accepted everything as truth and kept pushing through.

It wasn't until I discovered it wasn't *light* that was flashing that I became nervous, it was the *dark*, and moments later there was *only dark* and dark alone.

In a panic, I pulled on the hand with the pinched sleeve and applied enough pressure to tear the material free from the plane's grasp, causing me to fall slowly to the ground and bounce along the surface. Curiously, it seemed I was the *only* thing affected by the lunar conditions. As I struggled to pull myself to a standing position, I felt a pulsing vibration inside my pocket. It was my phone. Surely it was Kayla texting again, but inside the spacesuit I was unable to check. I wondered if she had seen the crash, though I doubted it, seeing as how the wreckage now stood in the shadows of the dark side of the moon. Perhaps she'd seen something on the news about it though. After all, how often does a Boeing 777 break through the earth's atmosphere and crash-land on the lunar surface without the media being all over it?

My wondering stopped suddenly as a blinding beam of light shined down upon me from somewhere deep in the darkness above. I turned my face to the ground to keep my eyes from burning out completely. The brightness was so incredibly intense it almost felt like a weight pushing down on me, trying to pin me against the ground. I felt trapped in a way, not unlike an insect burning in a beam of sunlight intensified through a magnifying glass. It felt like something was attempting to *exterminate* me. For a moment I welcomed it. I even considered stripping my suit and clothes to lay naked in the heat until either suffocating or burning to death, but as I turned to the wreckage, I caught a glimpse of something peculiar and had an overwhelming urge to investigate.

As the light beamed down on me, it also illuminated part of the plane, revealing two bodies strapped to chairs inside the cockpit. The bodies belonged to the pilots, and although they were still draped in their formal flight suits and caps, their skin and internal gore had vanished completely. Only their bare skeletons remained. I pulled myself to my feet and moon-stepped towards the wreckage. The spotlight followed me.

The passenger door of the plane had broken off, lost at some point during the crash, so getting inside was rather easy. It was dark on the inside, but not so dark it was impossible to see. The intensity of the spotlight was just enough that it leaked in through the windows, illuminating the passengers seated in the outer isles of the plane. Every passenger was also reduced to only a skeleton, as if they had all been dead for years. Perhaps just as unnerving, the passengers were all still seated, despite the terrible crash they'd all just experienced. Surely seatbelt technology wasn't so advanced that they were now able to keep bodies from flying out of their seats, despite the entire plane having been bent in half and split apart at the end. Something was wrong, at least it was finally starting to *feel* wrong to me.

It was at this moment I started to suspect I was dreaming, so I decided to test it. I'd always heard it was possible to awaken yourself within a dream by finding a light switch and flipping it on and off. I'd never tested the theory, but thought it was just as good a time as any to try it out. I walked down the left aisle of the plane, scanning the walls for a switch with no luck. I couldn't remember seeing a light switch inside a plane *ever*, at least in *real life*, so I wasn't sure I'd find one in whatever version of reality I seemed to be experiencing in the moment, but still I felt compelled to check regardless. The aisle began to curve upwards as I approached the mid-section of the plane, so much so I was unable to access the second half. Instead, I leapt upwards and grabbed onto a broken section of the floor, which stood vertically at this point, and heaved myself up until I was able to squeeze into the space below. Between the floor and the bottom of the plane, there was a space containing wires and electrical parts, so I thought if there was a switch to be found somewhere on the plane, it would be there. However, the search for the switch was quickly abandoned once I stumbled upon what very well could have been the reason the plane crashed in the first place—the battery.

It wasn't in great condition, that much was certain, though it wasn't immediately clear as to whether that was due to the wreck or something else that happened prior to the plane spinning out of control. It was a large box bolted to the undercarriage and all the surrounding wires and cables seemed to lead back into it. There was some sort of buildup around the cables that had a blue tint to it, most likely battery acid, and there were several large cracks that split the box in several sections on each side. Upon closer inspection, it appeared as though the battery itself, which I discovered was actually contained *within* the damaged box, was expanding, growing larger than the shell that contained it. There was a rhythmic pulse as it expanded, I noticed, as if the thing was breathing, or beating like a living heart. I pulled away a section of the steel box that was already knocked loose from the damage, a section that very curiously displayed the word "Pinky" across the length of it, and what was revealed on the inside turned out to be no battery at all, at least not in the sense I had initially thought—inside the box was living tissue, large pink and grey folds of it, an honest to god *living, pulsating brain.*

I pushed my gloved fingers against the flesh of the nerve ball and electricity instantly shot through my hand, took hold of my bones, and set my entire body on fire. I stumbled backwards in shock, tripped on one of the cables running into the box, and fell deep into a dark ocean.

I was no longer in control of my body. No matter how hard I tried, I could not get myself to move my arms or kick my legs. The surface of the water became farther away with every passing second as I sank deeper into the ocean, then for the second time during my trip, I'd become swallowed in darkness.

Out in the distance, thirteen orbs glowed in a variety of colors, and swam ever closer to me. They moved as if confused or perhaps drunk, dipping and spiraling outward in the water, then back towards me. Then, inexplicably, the little lights were suddenly naked women, swimming in circles around me, or at least that's how they appeared to me. My vision was quickly becoming blurred from the condensation collecting on the inside glass of the space helmet, so it was unclear if the orbs were ever even orbs at all. Perhaps at some point they had *morphed* into women, beautiful, if not a little thin, and curiously all equipped with the tails of large fish where there should have been legs.

Mermaids.

They said nothing to me, or if they had I could not hear it. The mermaids only seemed interested in the spacesuit I was wearing, which of course was something I doubt they had ever seen before. *How could they have?* They took hold of the material, studied it, and tugged gently at the arms and legs until each piece separated and swam out into the surrounding darkness. I could do nothing but watch as the creatures murdered me. Water immediately rushed inside, filling the spaces between the suit and my legs, abdomen, and breasts, and started to push its way into my helmet. Two of the mermaids unlatched the locks and pulled the helmet away, removing my only source of oxygen, and continued to pull at my clothing until there was absolutely nothing left.

I was naked and cradled in the arms of thirteen mermaids.

Somehow even my hair had become lost in the mix, as if just through their touch *poison* was released into my body causing every follicle of hair to die and fall away from my pale skin. I felt uncomfortable being so exposed and with the frigidness of the water and how each of the strange sea creatures were examining my body, looking at me as if I were some sort of vessel they could crawl inside, perhaps to procreate, my womb a nest for their eggs. As they swam around me, I noticed they all had the same wound, what looked to be rope burn in a ring around their necks. None of them seemed to be feeling any pain, so I assumed they must have been only scars, something from long ago, but of course I wasn't certain.

By then, some of them were running their tongues along my skin, as if they could taste the death that was creeping in. Others pushed needles into my flesh, syringes full of bright yellow liquid, glowing like pure electricity riding the skies, and feeling just the same as it coursed through my veins.

They sang my body electric.

A salty tongue parted my lips, and it was not my own. One of the creatures pushed her lips against mine and took hold of my tongue with her tongue, forcibly. The kiss did not feel like a kiss at all, instead it felt threatening, as if she was ready to rip the muscle clean from my mouth. It felt like a definite display of dominance, the alpha female silently commanding for me to submit to her and her sisters. I didn't resist. I couldn't, even if I wanted to. I remained paralyzed and at their mercy.

That's when I heard a voice, but not with my ears.

"Bricker, it's time to wake up," it said to me. The voice did not seem to be auditory, but rather telepathic. It was the mermaid. Her tongue had connected our nervous systems and she was sending messages directly to my brain.

"Bricker, you goddamn wolfcat."

The voice was familiar, a deep static-filled voice that didn't seem to be her own. It was definitely the voice of a man, a man that must have been part of my past. *Memories swirled...* Inexplicably, at least in the moment, the voice felt almost like my father's—*but he was not my father.*

"You've been wandering long enough. It's time to go," said the voice. Then the mermaid let loose of my tongue and swam away and the voice was no more.

My eye caught a glimpse of a large hook shining in the dark water above me and I followed it as it made its way down. The hook was attached to near invisible fishing line, but somehow it knew exactly where I was and how to get to me, as if it were equipped with some sort of homing device [or again it very well could have been that I was in a *dream*, but had no way of telling for sure]. One of the sisters grabbed hold of the hook, pushed the sharp end past the opening of my mouth, and pierced the inside of my jaw till the end of the hook jutted out about a half a foot from my face.

Consciousness was waning at this point and I was unsure if it was due to the lack of oxygen, the pain of the hook piercing through my skin, or from whatever it was the mermaids injected into my veins. My vision flickered like a strobe light as the hook pulled taut at my cheek. I was being pulled away from the grasp of the mermaids, and when my vision returned they again appeared only as glowing orbs to me. My eyes closed for what felt like an eternity, but very well could have only been minutes, seconds…

When I opened my eyes, Gordon was holding me by the skin of the neck, in the same place a mother cat would carry her young. He looked at me not with disappointment, but rather with intent, as if He was studying my face for clues. I remained silent, hanging there limply in his grasp—wet, hairless, and naked.

He threw me to the floor. It was only then that I noticed we were back on the bullet train, speeding through dark matter somewhere in outer space. He pointed to a bench that ran along the wall and told me to get dressed. Folded neatly at the end of the bench was a hospital gown. I unfolded it and wrapped it around my body. It annoyingly clung to the wetness of my skin. If given the choice between this and being naked, I would have stayed naked. However, I was not given a choice.

"Where are we?" I asked, surprised I was even able to speak.

Gordon turned away from me, and at first I thought He was not going to respond.

"Where are we? When are we? What are we? Who are we? Why are we? How are we?" He said.

I decided to sit down.

"We're headed for the edge of the universe," He said, after some silence.

"The edge? But there is no *edge* of the universe. It is without end, and constantly expanding," I said.

"No, there most certainly *is* an end," He said. "A *definite* and *abrupt* end. That's where we'll soon be."

I looked down at my feet and shook my head. I wasn't sure of what to say next. Gordon spun around angrily and before I could even process it, He was right in front of my face and screaming at me.

"So you think you've figured it out, huh?" He yelled. Spit leapt from His mouth and landed directly on my face. I didn't wipe it away or even flinch. "You know nothing! You've never known a damn thing!"

He took hold of my gown and pulled with great force, violently throwing me to the steel floor of the train. He pulled so hard the gown tore away from my body and remained clinched within His fist. I attempted to run from Him, but I panicked and tripped before I could ever fully get up on my feet. He stood over my quivering naked body and wrapped the ends of the gown over each of His fists.

"Let me teach you a little something, Bricker," He said, and as he spoke my name, the outer image of my body flickered from female to male, then back again. For just that split second, my breasts and vagina had disappeared, replaced instead with muscular pectorals and a dangling penis and testicles. It was a maddening thought, especially trying to make any sense of it, but I couldn't deny what I had just seen with my own two eyes.

He wrapped the gown around my neck and choked me out. I did not resist or try to push Him away. I was ready to go. My blood pressure felt as if it were doubling with every millisecond that passed, so much so it felt my head was going to blow right off my shoulders.

"Bricker, you goddamn wolverine," He said, and again I had morphed into a male. I reached down to take my penis into my hands, just to verify I wasn't hallucinating, but it appeared and disappeared all within a second. I felt around my groin looking for it, but found nothing except my female parts. Gordon looked down at my hands as I was examining myself. He seemed confused. He let up on the gown and I instinctively took in a large breath, sending myself into a terrible coughing fit.

"Is this bothering you?" He asked, pointing to my vagina. "Do you feel ashamed?"

I could not respond due to the coughing.

He stood up and walked over to the back of the train. I could hear Him fumbling through what sounded to be a mess of equipment, perhaps a toolbox of some sort. When He returned He had a roll of silver duct tape in His hand.

"This should help with that," He said, then proceeded to wrap the tape around my hips, covering my nakedness and more. By the time He was finished, I was tautly wrapped from my hips to my ankles, not unlike a mermaid. He then folded my arms over my breasts and taped them in place so I couldn't move. Again I was paralyzed.

"No," I finally managed to say.

"No what?" He asked.

"No, I do not feel ashamed."

He laughed.

"Well, you *should*. Do you have any idea what you've done?" He asked.

I wasn't sure what He was referring to and therefore could not respond.

"This cycle is over. I'm ending it," He said, then seemingly from out of nowhere, He heaved a large moon rock high over His head and came down on my skull with such force that pieces of my brain splattered all the way to the back of the train.

But. I. Lived. Through. It. All.

"*There is no end*," I said, with broken teeth and bleeding lips. "*It never ends.*"

"Bricker, my boy, it ends when I say it ends," He said. "This is all just a simulation within a simulation. If I want it finished, it shall be finished. I control *everything*, even the sun you see out there in the distance. It is all my creation. *Just watch...*"

And instantly the universe was dark and the sun was no more.

"If I want there to be light, there shall be light," He said.

And then there was light *and the light was good.*

"If I want to manipulate time to instantly turn you into a 163-year-old, I could do it faster than I could even snap my fingers. You and all the lives you know exist only in my creation, this simulation within a simulation. You are the *product*. You are the *experiment*. You are the *subject*. Your life has already been lived, spent, and now you are *forever dreaming*. Day after day the dreams return. They are cyclical and automatic. *Automated daydreaming.* All my creation. You are a *lie*. Nothing is *real*."

"Please kill me," I whimpered, unable to say anything more. I wanted nothing but to die, and more so than ever in that moment.

"I understand. After all, there are certainly things worse than death," He said. "But I can't let you go, Bricker. We still have so much more to explore and discover together. Don't you remember? *You wanted this.*"

"I wanted to escape," I said.

"You ingrate! What do you think this is?"

"I feel even deeper within the nightmare than I ever had before," I said. "This is no escape."

"You cannot get any further than you are—," He paused. "Right *now*."

As soon as He said this, the train stopped and the doors opened. Outside the doors there was a solitary white square, maybe ten feet by ten in size, surrounded by nothing but darkness.

"We've arrived at the edge of the universe, and at the edge, we do not speak," He said, then placed a strip of duct tape over my mouth.

My eyes rolled to the back of my head and suddenly I was visualizing myself in a field. The wind blew through the tall grass as I sat in a lawn chair, staring up at the night sky in total disgust. The moon would not kill me. My lunar suicide had failed. Again, I couldn't even do the work of a failure. *So what did that make me?*

Then I remembered what made that night bearable, and all nights, if I was being completely honest: *Kayla.* I thought about the last conversation we had together, and for the life of me I could not remember what it was. Then it occurred to me that I couldn't remember because I never responded to her last text. I hadn't even read it. Now my phone was lost somewhere deep within some strange dark sea and I would never get it back. I hadn't even the slightest idea of where to look. If I were to guess what it was she had said, my guess would be that it was short and simple, perhaps even a single word: *'goodbye.'*

    I muttered this word repeatedly to myself, muffled of course by the tape over my mouth, as I hanged there from the white square by the hospital gown wrapped around my neck. My bashed skull hung limply on my shoulder and blood dribbled from it, drops falling into the eternal nothingness below. I could do nothing but watch as the train pulled away, growing smaller with every second, until it disappeared completely. *Just watch, it was all I ever could do.*

    I was alone again.

    Alone and forever alive.

    The only thing more terrible than living this life, I'd imagine, would be discovering it was someone else's all along. *Was that what*

Gordon was suggesting when he said I was living in a simulation within a simulation?

Whatever he meant, he was right about one thing for sure: there were things far worse than death itself.

This much I was certain.

[32] If You Don't Sleep, You Don't Dream.

After watching through her eyes for several minutes, despite her crushed skull and blurred vision, I found myself becoming physically ill. I should have cut away from her story sooner. Her fate had me wondering about my own. Had he really been calling her Bricker, or had I only imagined it? Was this the first time, or had I only just noticed it? Had it been happening all along? I wasn't certain. I was so caught up in watching that I found I had temporarily lost my own sense of awareness. It wasn't until after switching channels that I had even realized the parallels between her life and all the others, my own included. I suppose there was always a certain danger in watching, that much I had anticipated from the beginning, however I couldn't get myself to abstain from these dangers. I found myself anxious to discover more. One more, I told myself, one more channel and then I'd go back to me. As much as it sickened me to do so, I clicked over to channel thirty-two and watched...

XVI

We are in a car.
Mary is driving.
I'm not exactly sure where we're going
but we're going there together.
I can't stop looking at her perfect skin
her green eyes.
Through her peripheral vision,
she notices me staring.
She smiles.
Without turning her head, she speaks.

Can I help you?

I smile.
She turns to look at me.
Mary's face ages thirty years in an instant.
Her body changes shape, her skin... her perfect skin,
hangs now in folds from her bones. Her hair thins, but her eyes, her beautiful green eyes are

still as young and full of life as I remember them.
It is then I realize I am daydreaming again.

Well?

Mary is still waiting for an answer.

You are... a very beautiful woman, Mary.

Her cheeks flush.
I don't know what I was thinking all those years ago.
Instead of following Gordon, I should have went after her.
I let the pain get to me.
I felt helpless.
The weight of guilt causes me to turn away from her.
I can't look at her now.
Our bodies are too old for sadness.
We've seen it all.
We're supposed to be stronger than this.
Our skin should be thicker than this.
But here we are... breaking down.

When we get to the prison gate, she tells me she is scared.
I hold her hand as the guard waves us through.

There is nothing I can do to heal the holes I've torn in both our hearts.
There is only [I squeeze her hand tightly] this moment.
And this moment... is nice.

We are sitting now in the visitor's room.
The heat is sweltering and I'm overdressed.
I have my face wrapped to hide my scarring and the hood of my jacket pulled over the back of my head.
Sweat starts to soak through the cloth covering my face and neck.

I'm not nervous.
Anxious, yes, but not nervous.
Mary is terrified, squeezing my hand with such strength my bones ache.
I say nothing.
Minutes later, he walks through the door.
Brogan Spivey.
I've never seen the bastard before today, but somehow I know him when I see him.
This man has haunted my dreams for nearly fifty years.
I could identify him by his smell alone.
He is exactly as I'd envisioned in my dreams.
Exactly.

He is an old man now, but still younger than the two of us.
Thin body, thin hair, thin skin... the handcuffs they have him in tear into his wrists.
He doesn't seem to notice.
He sits down in the booth across from us, and between us now is only glass.
He picks up the telephone receiver.
I look over at Mary.

Are you okay?

She has a terrified look on her face.

Yeah, it's just hard, you know?
I'll be okay.

I nod my head and pick up the receiver.
Spivey has a smirk I'd love to cut clean off his face.
Control.

So...

Spivey speaks into the receiver.

Who the hell are you people?

You killed our son, you bastard.

Seth Argyl.

Refresh my memory...

Refresh your memory?
How many children have you killed?

Twenty-seven....ish.

Jesus Christ! You fucking monster!

Well, this isn't where they keep gentlemen.

Spivey laughs.
Mary stands.
She's getting anxious.

Look, you abducted both of our children
while we were
vacationing at the beach.
Our daughter, she got away, but our son…
you killed our son.

Oh yeah, I remember your boy.
Whatever happened to that daughter of yours?
Is she still around? She was a cutie.

Now I'm standing.

> Listen you crazy bastard,
> we only came here today for closure.
> We want to know where you buried
> our son's body.

Spivey chuckles at this request.

> *You want to know where I buried your son's body?*
> *Well... that's easy. I didn't.*

> What? What do you mean?

> *I mean, I ate your boy.*

Shock floods my system and rage takes full control of my body.
I throw my chair through the glass window, the only thing separating us from that killer, that murderer of children!
I thrust my right arm out, and a twelve-inch blade tears through the skin of my wrist from within me.
A weapon of Gordon's design!
I leap through to the other side, gouging the blade through Spivey's windpipe.
Prison guards rush in and try to pin me to the floor.
I release the blade in my left arm and rampage through all that surround me...

...including Mary.

When there is nothing left to kill, my rage finally settles.
At this moment I am not human.
I have become something different entirely.

XVII

A disgrace!
A poor excuse for a living, breathing soul, I am!
I've killed people!
There's blood on my hands!
I'm powerful, but fucking weak!
I can't control my rage!
I'm a beast, not a man.
I'm running away again...
I'm going to Hell.
I'm leaving this world, again for the comfort of Gordon's protective wing.
I run along the wet streets, making my way to Steen Boneyard.
I see a pay phone.
Stop. Breathe. Dial.
I am terrified, defeated, and alone.

An innocent voice funnels down my ear canal.
Mary's voice. A recording. Voicemail.
Her voice stings me.
My broken ear must suffer this.
BEEP.
I speak in a voice unlike my own.
I speak in a voice swollen with sadness.

                        Mary... I am sorry.
                      I don't belong here.
                I don't belong here, Mary!
Adam Argyl died that night on the beach...
                              with his son.
                 Mary... Adam is gone.
               It's just me, Lazarus, now.
            Gordon, He gave me this life...
I wanted to escape, but he gave me this
    and took away all I've ever loved.
          ETERNAL LIFE, MARY.
       A curse, it is! A goddamn curse!
              To watch my loves die.
        To live forever is to live alone.
         I'm leaving, this time for good.
        And Joan... if you're listening...
            Know that I love you...
And know that this is the only way I can ever
                              show you.
       I'm so sorry about your mother.
                      I'm so sorry.

I hang up the phone and find myself standing before the graveyard.
A familiar figure is brooding along the edge of the fountain of Poseidon.
Gordon.
He welcomes me home.

XVIII

Hell is cold, dark.
Water trembles faintly down the walls and glitters when it finds light.
The air is thick with mold.
The clean air beyond the surface must have spoiled my lungs.
Gordon and I weave through a labyrinth of pipe and wall, finally reaching our destination: the warehouse.
In my time with Gordon, the warehouse had only served one purpose: it was the breeding ground, the room He used to manufacture human life.
But instead of rows of naked women held up in stirrups, there are now rows of uniformed soldiers.

> *Well, what do you think, Laz, my boy?*
> *Isn't it exactly as you dreamed?*

Gordon speaks as if we never missed a step.
As if the death of my son and my wife do not tear at my heartstrings.
As if their deaths could not possibly cause me to turn away from him.

Or maybe that is it?
Maybe Gordon again sees the fire that burned in me
so long ago?
It certainly feels as if it has returned.

I look around the room at all the bodies, young men and women.
Some covered with fresh scars.

> You did it, Gordon...
> You've created your army.
> There must be thousands here.

> *144,000 to be exact.*
> *It only took me thirty years.*
> *Jesus, Lazarus, we're old men now.*
> *Look at us... brilliant and strong.*
> *And to think, in just ten short hours...*
> *the world will be ours!*

He is ready.
His army is ready.
Oceans of blood will flood the Earth when
He is finished.

Gordon... where do I fit into... the plan?

*Attach your wings and bring your marvelous blades
down upon the world.
Make them feel your pain.
Just like that day on the highway so many years ago...
Do you remember that day?*

Yes.

Do you still feel that same hatred within you?

Yes.

*Do more than just feel it... act on it.
Slit the throat of every man, woman, and child,
for a superior race is born!*

But, Gordon... only sinners, right?

*They are ALL sinners!
Every last goddamn one of them!*

> But, Gordon... this isn't the plan...
> We punish only the wicked.

THEY. ARE. ALL. WICKED.

Let God pass judgment on them.

> I AM GOD!

Gordon grabs my throat, digging His nails deep.

> I... am... God.

Gordon tosses me aside like a rag doll,
then picks my flesh out from beneath His fingernails.

> *It's your daughter, isn't it?*
> *You want to save her.*

Yes... will you spare her life?

Gordon looks into my eyes.
He's become a different man.
He sees me now as a stranger.

> *No.*

*No life shall be spared.
But... I am willing to make you a deal.*

Yes, anything...

I need you to implant this inside my brain.

Gordon holds up a contraption much like the spider implant, but far more advanced.
I've never seen such a complicated device before.
I'm not even sure of its primary functions.
However, I do know how to install it.
Gordon has trained me well.
I'm the only person, other than Himself, with this knowledge.
He needs me.

And in return?

In return... I'll let you get a head start.

A head start?

I'll let you try to find your daughter, but know this, once we find her, we will stop her heart. So enjoy these last few moments with her, Laz. I promise you, it's all you've got.

I take the deal.
I must find Joan.
The operation is at least a seven-hour procedure.
That leaves me with only three hours to find Joan and bring her to safety.
I waste no time.

An hour into the operation and a question enters and distracts my mind:
Why don't I kill Gordon right here on this table?
His brain is exposed.
He is at my mercy!
I can put an end to this all!
But Gordon is too clever to allow it.
It seems all of his creations have been implanted with a small chip that disables rage within a certain range of him, and I am no exception.
My hands are of no use, other than to operate.

It takes a full eight hours to complete the operation.
As soon as Gordon is sewed up,
I run like hell.

XIX

Joan is inside her house.
She refuses to come with me.
She is yelling and screaming at me through the door.
I've mistakenly murdered her mother, my wife, and she'd been informed by the police no more than an hour before my visit.
I try to warn her about *the war*.
She is screaming obscenities, claiming the police are 'on their way.'
I try everything to get her to come with me.

> *Why, so you can rape me like you raped all those other women? What the fuck is wrong with you?*

She screams in a fit.
My heart breaks.
Sadly, I have no choice but to leave her,
but before I go, I force a blade out through my wrist and carve a map into her door.
The directions lead to the only place in the world where I know we will be safe: the original underground warehouse.
It has been abandoned for over two decades now.

Gordon will not look for us there.
I hope Gordon will not look for us there.

The old warehouse is exactly as I remember it.
Gordon hardly took anything.
Papers are still stacked high on His desk, cabinets, furniture all in place, albeit covered in a thick layer of dust.

I walk into the control room, flip a switch.
The surveillance monitors all seem to be intact.
All six of them.
The cameras are all hidden in various places, up on the surface.
Gordon has always been paranoid of being caught, raided by the law, before His attack was ready.
Twenty-three years ago, this was the best surveillance system on the market.
Top dollar and well worth it.
Now, not so much, but it will do.
I continue my tour throughout the warehouse.
Memories are fading in and out.
There are a lot of lost years—

An earthshaking explosion sounds from above.
Soon followed by another.
I run to the control room and take a look at the

surveillance monitors.
I watch as Gordon's army slaughters people on the surface.
Bodies are ripped in two and thrown aside.
Their entrails are scattered across the pavement and hanging from tree branches.
I turn off the cameras and vomit on the floor.
Faintly, a voice calls for me.

Dad?

I turn around and Joan is standing in the doorway.

Joan!

Tears stream down her cheeks as she reaches out for me.
We embrace.
This time I don't try to calm her.

XX

It's been quiet for an hour now.
Joan has fallen asleep.

I've been sitting here, next to her, trying to build up enough courage to turn the surveillance monitors back on.
Finally, I stand and walk into the control room. I take a deep breath before flipping the switch. It appears that four of the cameras have been destroyed, their monitors displaying only static. The other two monitors are fogged by what appears to be clouds of dust.
The fog is so thick that I'm unable to see anything.
I turn the monitors off again.

Hands to face, I take in another deep breath.
I have to know if it's over.
The silence is causing my skin to tremble.

I open the hatch and walk out onto the surface. The dust clouds sting my eyes and fill my lungs. The sun is setting and casting the strangest colors upon the land: purple and green.
It's as if the sun is dying.
The wind begins to slow a bit and some of the dust settles to the earth.
Finally I am able to see the aftermath:

Everything in sight is dead.

[41] NOSEBLEED/ CABLEJUICE

- Part Two -

I thought I had awakened from my deep slumber for a sliver of a second, but my eyes never actually opened. I could hear sounds and movement as someone or something walked around me, tinkering with what sounded to be small metal objects near my ears. No matter how hard I tried, I could not open my eyes. I assumed I must have still been asleep, still dreaming.
One final dream(?) came to me...

There was a room, a cold room with white tiled flooring. The tiles were stained pink from the blood running off the table located in the center of the room, collecting in puddles on the floor. There was a body lying on the table, a man's body, but the head and been emptied [cut open like a melon with the insides scraped clean out], so I could not tell who it was.

I was not in this room, or so I thought at the time. I assumed I was dreaming I was someone else, as I often do, but strangely I could not see myself. Even as I looked down to examine, looking for my body, for flesh and blood, there was nothing. I was no one, only a vapor, or so it seemed.

There was another man in the room, a man dressed in all grey. His face was hidden behind a surgical mask. His eyes were filled with white [no irises, no pupils, just white]. He held a large object in his hands, a jar, half-filled with some dark blue-colored liquid. Something about the jar made him chuckle, soft at first, but quickly escalated into hearty laughs, deep and guttural. He walked over to a tray sitting on the table next to the hollow-headed body. The tray was filled with what I assumed to be the contents of the hollow-headed man's skull. The man in grey, still sniggering, proceeded to stuff the jar full of the bloody offal from the tray in a violent, messy manner. The blue-colored liquid now appeared clouded and purple. A pair of eyeballs, a tongue, ears, and a brain were clearly visible within the glass walls of the jar, all crammed and piled on top of one another like cucumbers in a pickle jar.

Bricker, you're a goddamn wolverine. I heard a voice say to me. *You can't teach your tricks to anyone. No, son, you were born with it. You're a goddamn wolfcat.*

The voice was not coming from the man in grey, the only man within an earshot of me, whoever and wherever I may have been at that moment. It was coming from deep within me, the demon inside my earhole.

The man in grey is xxxxxx. I warned you about Him.

I told you not to share your gifts with anyone, you goddamn fool. You are a man, alone. Always alone. People only slow you down.

I could not respond, instead I thought about the many lives I'd lived and tried imagining having lived them alone, without a single living soul hanging around my neck at any point. The demon was right. Other people only made my life more difficult. All my sadness, guilt, and unhappiness stemmed from the loss of individuals I had allowed myself to get close to.

Your purpose was different than what you made your fate. You realize this, don't you? Bricker, you goddamn wildebeest, you are an error, a glitch, and you are to blame for making yourself that way.

I wanted nothing more than to scream at the top of my lungs. I wanted to ask the demon the point of living five lives [or even one life, for that matter] if I am meant to live them all in isolation, abstinent of love, of desire, of passion. What was the point of life with those things removed?

You. Could. Have. Lived. Forever.

Is life worth living if you have no one to share your happiness with? Wouldn't those short-lived happy moments ultimately lead to massive periods of great sadness?

Your gifts were wasted on human invention, Bricker. You and all the others...

Others? There are others? Other what? Others... like me? I could not actually ask the demon these questions, having no mouth in which to speak, but I soon found I didn't need to. The answers appeared to waiting for me in the next room.

Bum. Bum. Bum-Bum-Bum.

The demon was drumming in my ear again. The closer I got to the doorway, the faster and more vigorous the drumming became. I felt a part of its song, as if I were musical notes dancing atop a wicked drumhead.

You're learning secrets, dear boy...

I stepped into the room. There were four other bodies stripped naked and lying on tables. Two were women and two were men. Blood dripped from craters that used to contain brains, eyeballs, the gore behind faces, and pooled on the floor beneath them. It was the scene from room one, but multiplied by four.

Five immortals, five jars, five channels. Turn around, Bricker.

I turned around. The man in grey, His white eyes burning images into mine [specters, ghosts] was standing before me. xxxxxx. He held up the jar so I could see it. The eyeballs inside were twitching, as if in REM cycle. There was a label stuck to the glass. It read, "Channel// Forty-One." He chuckled, turned, and placed the jar on the desk near a computer monitor. There were four other jars on the desk, all sporting the same gory contents. xxxxxx pulled two wires from behind the monitor and pushed them down into the jar labeled "Channel//Forty-One," piercing the brain flesh in two pinpoints, carefully placed.

Once the wires were in position, He spun His body around and pulled the surgical mask from His face. His mouth was open. He laughed maniacally. Television static liquefied and filled His mouth, leaking out the corners and dripping down onto His chest. Splashes of it were spat from His mouth with every wicked cackle. He held a finger high in the air, almost comically, like a cartoon or something. A strange sensation of dread came over me as I realized in that moment what was about to happen.

Bricker, you goddamn wolfcat.

With one final snigger [the static spewed from his mouth like vomit], He slammed His finger down on the computer keyboard and instantly the room disappeared.

When I awakened, I found myself standing at the edge of a plane, dressed in full uniform, struggling to find the courage to leap...

William Pauley III lives in Lexington, KY. You don't know him, and you don't know anyone who does.

Other books published by DOOM FICTION*

#006_*If You Don't Sleep, You Don't Dream.*
By William Pauley III

#005_*White Fuzz*
by William Pauley III

#004_*Demolition Ya Ya*
by William Pauley III

#003_*Automated Daydreaming*
by William Pauley III

#002_*The Naked Brunch*
by William Pauley III & Zachary T. Owen

#001_*Hearers of the Constant Hum*
by William Pauley III

*Despite the name, most likely you will
<u>not</u> be harmed by Doom Fiction.

www.doomfiction.com